SYLVIA PLATH

WITHDRAWN

Related titles from Palgrave Macmillan

Claire Brennan, *The Poetry of Sylvia Plath*
Linda Wagner-Martin, *Sylvia Plath: A Literary Life* (second edition)

Sylvia Plath

An Introduction to the Poetry

Second Edition

Susan Bassnett

First edition published 1987
Second edition published 2005 by
PALGRAVE MACMILLAN
Houndmills, Basingstoke, Hampshire RG21 6XS and
175 Fifth Avenue, New York, N.Y. 10010
Companies and representatives throughout the world

PALGRAVE MACMILLAN is the global academic imprint of the Palgrave Macmillan division of St. Martin's Press, LLC and of Palgrave Macmillan Ltd. Macmillan® is a registered trademark in the United States, United Kingdom and other countries. Palgrave is a registered trademark in the European Union and other countries.

ISBN 0–333–77127–3 hardback
ISBN 0–333–77126–5 paperback

This book is printed on paper suitable for recycling and made from fully managed and sustained forest sources.

A catalogue record for this book is available from the British Library.

A catalog record for this book is available from the Library of Congress.

10   9   8   7   6   5   4   3   2   1
14 13 12 11 10 09 08 07 06 05

Printed in China

Contents

Acknowledgements

I am grateful to Janet Bailey for her tireless help in preparing the manuscript, and to Sonya Barker for her infinite patience. Anna Sandeman and Kate Wallis have provided excellent advice and I have endeavoured to incorporate the many helpful suggestions offered by my colleagues and students, without whom this book would not have been written.

Introduction

Sylvia Plath is one of the best-known women poets of the twentieth century. Her fame has eclipsed even that of great, world-famous female poets, such as the Russian Anna Akhmatova, or Gabriela Mistral, the Chilean writer who won the Nobel prize for Literature in 1945. Yet unlike those poets, whose international reputations were established during their lifetime, Plath's fame came more slowly, growing gradually after her death in 1963 to the point where, at the end of the century, she had acquired an almost mythical status, inspiring dozens of biographies, critical studies, memoirs, performances and even, by 2003, a Hollywood film about her life, with Gwyneth Paltrow playing Sylvia.

The rise of Plath to this iconic status has been rapid. In the aftermath of her death, she was first seen as a relatively minor though gifted poet, overshadowed by the powerful poetry of her husband, Ted Hughes. Early responses to her poetry focussed on its darkness, on the imagery of blood and violence that appeared to prefigure her eventual suicide. Later, her work was reassessed, particularly by feminist critics, who drew attention to the power of her language, to the expressions of rage and outrage that run through her writing and to the way in which her work can be seen as exemplifying many of the contradictions and dilemmas faced by women struggling for self-realisation while endeavouring to conform to social expectations. While some critics read into Plath's work the story of a damaged individual whose death was the culmination of a long flirtation with the idea of dying, others saw her as an Everywoman, whose poetry spoke of the pain of being a women struggling to live up to impossible ideals of womanliness.

The diversity of opinion as to the quality of Sylvia Plath's poetry and the insistence of so many commentators to read her work as autobiographical have led to a proliferation of books, articles, documentaries and personal memoirs, many of which have been criticised by her family as contributing to what some see as a Plath exploitation industry. When the first edition of this book came out, in 1987, as a volume in a series of introductions to women writers, that industry was only just starting, and even a quick glance at the number of Plath studies produced over the last two decades shows how rapidly

interest in her has grown. Today, her poetry, the *Ariel* collection
in particular, and her novel, *The Bell Jar* are studied in secondary
schools and universities and her life story continues to fascinate
non-specialists.

Because Plath wrote in a highly individualistic way, developing
her own private mythology through the use of keywords and symbols,
weaving together themes and images in ways that are not always
immediately obvious to the reader, she has often been seen as a
'difficult' poet. Many of the studies of her writing seek to make
connections with episodes in her life, and it is certainly true that on
one level, Plath was a strongly autobiographical writer. Nevertheless,
as she insisted and as Ted Hughes has always argued, she did not
see poetry primarily as a conduit for her personal feelings, but rather
as a conscious process of crafting through which experience and
emotion could be refined in an alchemical sense and transformed
into something new. Hers is a poetry about searching for identity, and
part of that search was to find a voice as a writer and experiment
with the craft of poetry.

This book offers an introduction to that alchemical process, tracing
ideas and imagery that run through Plath's poetry. The structure is
only loosely chronological, since the primary aim is to show how
Plath's writing changed and developed, and how she reworked
particular thematic and linguistic patterns, rather than to argue that
the poems mirror every stage in her life-story. The poems are not
analysed so much as keys to a life, rather as readings that focus on
Plath's artistry and skills as a writer, relying on many of her own
statements about the nature and meaning of writing. Nevertheless,
because of the deliberate way in which Plath the poet transformed
elements of her experience through writing, a brief account of her
biography is provided.

For many years after Plath's death, Ted Hughes, her husband,
was accused, not only of having abandoned her and precipitated
her death, but also of having exercised control over her writing.
He admitted destroying some of her last work, on the grounds that
it would have caused too much pain for their children, but it was
Hughes who put together the edition of Sylvia Plath's *Collected
Poems* that won the Pulitzer Prize in 1981, and for the rest of his life,
until his death in 1998, Hughes defended both his own and Plath's
reputation and insisted on his family's right to privacy. He refused
to give any public account of his relationship with his dead wife,
though was occasionally goaded into angry rebuttals of particularly

painful accusations. Then, shortly before his death, Hughes published *Birthday Letters*, a collection of poems in which he broke his long silence and wrote about the years with Plath.

The final chapter of this book focusses on *Birthday Letters*. The inclusion of a chapter on poems by Ted Hughes in a book about Sylvia Plath might be seen as controversial, but the reason for its inclusion is that *Birthday Letters* is, effectively, a collection of poems in which Plath's poetry is translated by another poet. Hughes' intimate knowledge of Plath's writing led him to write poems that can be read in counterpoint to Plath's own work, so that *Birthday Letters* can be used as an important tool to aid understanding of her poetry as well as of his. Hughes' reading of Plath's poems, a subjective interpretation that translates her work for another generation of readers, serves as a conclusion to this introductory study of the poetry of an extraordinary writer.

1

Tracing a Life

In one of the first entries in her Journal, written in the summer of 1950 when she was eighteen years old, Sylvia Plath recorded her thoughts about being a writer and about her relationship as a writer with the world:

> I love people. Everybody. I love them, I think, as a stamp collector loves his collection. Every story, every incident, every bit of conversation is raw material for me. My love's not impersonal, yet not wholly subjective either. I would like to be everyone, a cripple, a dying man, a whore, and then come back to write about my thoughts, my emotions as that person.[1]

In the next entry, she wrote about the need to live fully in the world, to live in the present and added the phrase 'I don't want to die'. Despite the endeavours of so many people to read her work as a litany of despair and desire for death, it is important to balance this interpretation with her own written statements. What Sylvia Plath wanted was to experience life to the full, she wanted to be more than one person or, since she was compelled by necessity to live inside one body, she wanted to bring into that entity as many diverse experiences as possible. Hence her refusal to make choices between career and family, as was expected of women of her generation.

Nor should her writing be seen just as a series of confessional statements, for throughout her short life she followed the wish expressed in the passage above: she was fascinated by people, and recorded details of their appearance, conversations, actions in her Journals, and she endeavoured through the use of the I-speaker to enter into different consciousnesses and different worlds. In the poem 'Paralytic', for example, she speaks through the voice of an old, paralysed man:

> Photographs visit me –
> My wife, dead and flat, in 1920 furs,
> Mouth full of pearls

4

In 'Gigolo', written on the same day, in January 1963, the I-speaker proclaims:

> I shall never grow old. New oysters
> Shriek in the sea and I
> Glitter like Fontainebleau.

In poems such as these, Sylvia Plath experiments with characters, endeavouring to write as different people, even though at the same time she was also writing powerful poems in the first person that came directly from her own experiences.

Given the way in which she transformed her own life into writing, it is important to an understanding of her work to have some sense of her background, of the story of a star student, an all-American golden girl of the 1950s who fell in love with one of the greatest English poets of the twentieth century, moved across the Atlantic, suffered agonies when her ideal marriage collapsed and died finally by her own hand.

1932–55: THE AMERICAN YEARS

Sylvia Plath was born at Robinson Memorial Hospital in Boston on 27 October 1932, the first child of Otto and Aurelia Plath. Her father had come to the United States at the age of fifteen from the eastern area of Germany known then as the Polish Corridor and had become professor of biology at Boston University, specialising in ornithology, entomology and ichthyology. Two years after Sylvia's birth he published a treatise on *Bumblebees and their Ways* and critics have never been slow to point out the recurrence of bee imagery in Sylvia Plath's poetry, seeing this as a link with her father. Aurelia Plath, her mother, had been born in Boston of Austrian parents and had met her husband whilst studying for a Masters degree in English and German. Of their marriage, Aurelia Plath says little but what she does say is significant. She notes that her husband insisted on her giving up her teaching post after marriage, to become 'a full-time home-maker' and comments also that 'social life was almost nil for us as a married couple'.[2]

After Sylvia's birth, when Otto was working on his bumblebee book, the picture that emerges from Aurelia Plath's account is of a husband and wife moving rapidly in different directions:

The age difference between us (twenty-one years), Otto's superior education, his long years of living in college dormitories or rooming for himself, our former teacher–student relationship, all made this sudden change to home and family difficult for him, and led to an attitude of 'rightful' dominance on his part. He had never known the free-flow of communication that characterised my relationship with my family, and talking things out and reasoning together just didn't operate. At the end of my first year of marriage, I realised that if I wanted a peaceful home – and I did – I would simply have to become more submissive, although it was not my nature to be so.

Two-and-a-half years later (Aurelia Plath claims that Otto wanted a son born two and a half years to the day following Sylvia's birth and that she conveniently obliged with a baby on 27 April 1935), Sylvia's brother Warren was born. There were to be no other children. By 1936 Otto Plath had become ill, first it was thought, with cancer but later diagnosed as diabetes. He died in 1940 and Aurelia Plath describes in very brief terms the difficulties of nursing him whilst bringing up two small energetic children:

> I kept an 'upstairs-downstairs' household when both Otto and the children were indoors; partly so their noisy play and squabbling would not upset him, but mostly so that he would not frighten them, for he now occasionally suffered intense spasms in his leg muscles, which would cause him to moan in pain.

After Otto's death, Aurelia took up the strands of her life again, found a job and moved house, leaving the seaside town of Winthrop Massachusetts for Wellesley, a Boston suburb described by Lois Ames as being both conservative and upper middle-class.[3] Aurelia Plath, however, describes the new Plath home as being in a modest section of the town with low rates. She also notes that Wellesley College, which offered scholarships to students living in the town, 'might in the future hold opportunity for Sylvia'.

Biographical critics have made much of the move away from the sea at an early stage of Sylvia's life, of her reactions to her father's death, of her resentment towards her mother. Aurelia was aware of that resentment and notes that Sylvia failed to understand the way in which she coped with bereavement:

What I intended as an exercise in courage for the sake of my children was interpreted years later by my daughter as indifference. 'My mother never had time to mourn my father's death'. I had vividly remembered a time when I was a little child, seeing my mother weep in my presence and feeling that my whole personal world was collapsing. *Mother*, the tower of strength, my one refuge, *crying*! It was this recollection that compelled me to withhold my tears until I was alone in bed at night.

In this rather sad little moment of self-justification, a pattern of cyclical behaviour emerges: Aurelia's mother had created an image of herself as superwoman that Aurelia felt compelled to repeat for her own children. But whereas the woman from one generation might have been appalled at the sight of her mother breaking down, the woman from another generation would perhaps have welcomed it as a sign of honest emotion openly expressed. In the mother–daughter cycle the lines of communication continued to be confused down through the generations.

The picture depicted by Aurelia Plath of the early years of Sylvia's life is her own subjective viewpoint. Reading that account, we may be struck by the image she paints of Otto as a rigid man, with problems about expressing his feelings for other people, of herself as professionally frustrated but with great hopes for her daughter, of Sylvia as a child with whom she believed she could communicate closely, albeit not always through spoken words:

Both Sylvia and I were more at ease in *writing* words of appreciation, admiration, and love than in expressing these emotions verbally and, thank goodness, write them to each other we did!

In 1950, Sylvia graduated from Bradford High School and won a scholarship to Smith College. In the same year, she published a short story 'And Summer Will Not Come Again' in *Seventeen* and a poem, 'Bitter Strawberries', in *The Christian Science Monitor*. Three years later, she won a fiction contest sponsored by *Mademoiselle* and described the sense of euphoria she felt:

After being one of the two national winners of Mademoiselle's fiction contest (500)! Last August, I felt that I was coming home again when I won a guest editorship representing Smith & took a train to NYC for a salaried month working – hatted and heeled – in

Mile's air-conditioned Madison Ave. offices...Fantastic, fabulous, and all other inadequate adjectives go to describe the four gala and chaotic weeks I worked as guest managing ed.[4]

But after the euphoria came a swing of mood in the opposite direction. Writing to her brother Warren in late June 1953, she describes her sense of exhaustion and world-weariness. Aurelia Plath was faced with the job of telling her that she had not been accepted as a student in Frank O'Connor's writing class, a fact which she feels deepened Sylvia's depression. That depression grew worse and in August she tried to commit suicide by swallowing a bottle of sleeping pills. She was found later by her brother and taken to hospital, where she spent several months undergoing psychiatric treatment and, eventually, electric shock treatment as well. The account of the breakdown and suicide attempt and subsequent recovery in hospital that forms the basis of her later novel, *The Bell Jar*, was based on first-hand experience. In Chapter 20, Esther recalls her mother's visit in the following terms:

> Doctor Nolan had said, quite bluntly, that a lot of people would treat me gingerly, or even avoid me, like a leper with a warning bell. My mother's face floated to mind, a pale, reproachful moon, at her last and first visit to the asylum since my twentieth birthday. A daughter in an asylum! I had done that to her. Still, she had obviously decided to forgive me.

'We'll take up where we left off, Esther,' she had said, with her sweet, martyr's smile. 'We'll act as if all this were a bad dream.'
A bad dream.
To the person in the bell jar, blank and stopped as a dead baby, the world itself is the bad dream.
A bad dream.
I remembered everything.[5]

In 1954, Sylvia returned to Smith College, subsequently winning several poetry competitions. She wrote her undergraduate thesis on Dostoevsky, entitled 'The Magic Mirror: A Study of the Double in Two of Dostoevsky's Novels'. She graduated *summa cum laude* and went on to win a Fulbright scholarship to Cambridge. Throughout this period her letters show that she was continually writing and sending off manuscripts to publishers. In a letter to her mother on 2 February 1955, she wrote about the impact of rejections on her:

I begin to feel that I lack that 'indefinable something' that makes a winner...
Now I can see the advantage of an agent – she keeps you from the little deaths every writer goes through whenever a manuscript comes back home. It's like having your child refused admittance to public school. You love it, and often can't see why.

But also, in the same letter, she described a change in her writing:

I have felt great advances in my poetry, the main one being a growing victory over word nuances and a superfluity of adjectives.

Sylvia Plath was about to move on into another phase of development. The end of the time at Smith College as a student marked the start of her next stage, as a student across the ocean in England. Her subsequent meeting there with Ted Hughes was to have enormous impact on her, both in terms of her writing and her private life. The poem she wrote in the summer of 1955, 'The Princess and the Goblins', read in retrospect, seems almost prophetic:

> From fabrication springs the spiral stair
>   up which the wakeful princess climbs to find
>   the source of blanching light that conjured her
> to leave her bed of fever and ascend
>   a visionary ladder toward the moon
>   whose holy blue anoints her injured hand.

1955–59: THE TRANSATLANTIC YEARS

At Cambridge, Sylvia Plath settled into a new routine, bringing a particularly American perspective to what she experienced. The letters home give ample evidence of this perspective; on hearing lectures by F. R. Leavis she describes him as 'a magnificent, acid, malevolently humorous little man who looks exactly like a bandy-legged leprechaun' (9 October 1955); she comments further on Cambridge academics:

I see in Cambridge, particularly among the women dons, a series of such grotesques! It is almost like a caricature series from Dickens to see our head table at Newnham. Daily we rather merciless and merry Americans, South Africans, and Scottish students remark the types at the dons' table, which range from a tall, cadaverous woman with purple hair (really!) to a midget Charles Adams fat creature who has to stand on a stool to get into the soup tureen. They are all very brilliant or learned (quite a different thing) in their specialised ways, but I feel that all their experience is *secondary* (*second-hand*?) and this to me is tantamount to a kind of living death. (22 November 1955)

A short while later she talks about having tea with Chris Levenson and discusses the practice of English critics:

It seems this is an age of clever critics who keep bewailing the fact that there are no works worthy of criticism. They abhor polished wit and neat forms, which, of course, is exactly what I purpose to write, and when they criticize something for being 'quaintly artful' or 'merely amusing', it is all I can do not to shout, 'That's all I meant it to be!' (2 February 1956)

Adjusting to English life was a complex matter. At times she writes about the excitement of living so near to the rest of Europe, feeling on the brink of the rest of the civilised world, as it were, but after a trip to France in the winter of 1955–56 she came back to the English dampness dispirited. The climate in Cambridge is a constant subject of her letters, as is the 'atrocious food'. Not long after her arrival, she wrote to her mother trying to express the feeling of rootlessness she was experiencing:

Perhaps what I do miss most here is the lack of my friends who have known me in my past. I can't explain fully how much it means to have people who have shared years of one's life and with whom you can assume a deep understanding and common experience.... (14 November 1955)

What Sylvia Plath seems to have been experiencing was the realisation of the vast differences between American and English culture. Ostensibly similar, in view of the common language, the two cultures are distanced by vast unbridgeable differences. Describing the smallness of British literary circles, Sylvia Plath remarks 'Blessed be

America for its catholic *bigness*!' The charm and quaintness of life in London or Cambridge could not altogether compensate for the loss of familiar patterns of behaviour and for the rich mixture of tastes and habits that made up life in America. As an American in England she was inevitably marginalised; not belonging to the culture in which she found herself, looking at England and the English with the eyes of an outsider. And just as the physical grotesqueness of Cambridge intellectuals struck her as memorable, so in one of her poems specifically about Cambridge, 'Watercolour of Grantchester Meadows', she uses metaphor to point to the contrast between appearance and reality that seems at the heart of English life:

> It is a country on a nursery plate.
> Spotted cows revolve their jaws and crop
> Red clover or gnaw beetroot
> Bellied on a nimbus of sun-glazed buttercup.
> Hedging meadows of benign
> Arcadian green
> The blood-berried hawthorn hides its spines with white.
>
> 19 February 1959

It is perhaps fitting that this poem, which she describes in her Journal as 'bucolic' should have been accepted by the *New Yorker* – an American's English poem for American readers. But the sense of cultural displacement was not only linked to nationality. In her short essay 'America! America!', published in *Punch* in April 1963, hence written for British readers, she describes the American dream of social equality achieved through education. Tracing her own academic career through the American public school system into college, describing the absurd rites of the sorority to which she belonged, Plath ends up by stating her own sense of not-belonging:

> Somehow it didn't take – this initiation into the nihil of belonging. Maybe I was too weird to begin with ... The privilege of being anybody was turning its other face to the pressure of being every-body; ergo, no one.[6]

And the essay concludes with an ironic comparison between the clean, shiny look of a new American primary school and her own recollection of 'anarchism, discomfort and grit', noting the shift in emphasis that has mystified and delayed processes of reading whereas 'my lot did it by age four off soapbox tops'. Plath ends the essay with a question; but a question that is not only directed to the discussion of American primary education. 'Did I glimpse, in the First Aid cabinet, a sparkle of bottles – soothers and smootheners for the embryo rebel, the artist, the odd?' she asks, implying that education serves rather to muffle exceptional creativity than to allow it a free speaking voice.

It was at Cambridge, in February 1956, that Sylvia Plath met Ted Hughes. Her Journal records the meeting, describing it in terms of noise and violence – 'We shouted as if in a high wind'; 'I stamped and screamed'; and in a letter to her mother of 3 March, she writes about Hughes that he is 'the only man I've met yet here who'd be strong enough to be equal with'. They married four months later, on 16 June.

The letters written between 3 May 1956 and 17 June 1957 have been collected together into one section of *Letters Home* and are described by Aurelia Plath as 'radiant letters, when love and a complete sharing of hopes and dreams acknowledge no limits'. Certainly many of the letters bear witness to Sylvia Plath's expression of happiness, her enormous enthusiasm for Ted Hughes' writing, her love for him and her sense of unity with him, though the Journal is more ambiguous and offers a glimpse of her feelings of ambiguity in the spring of 1956 when she went on a visit to Paris. Nevertheless, by summer, in the first enthusiastic weeks of the marriage spent wandering round France and Spain, what comes across from reading her letters is a sense of her exuberance at being the 'wife of the internationally known poet and genius' (letter to Warren, 18 June). What they shared, apart from love for each other, was the drive to write and to publish; as the last line of her poem 'Wreath for a Bridal' promises: 'Let flesh be knit, and each step hence go famous'.

Margaret Uroff, in her book *Sylvia Plath and Ted Hughes*, has looked at the work of both poets comparatively, searching for the influences each may have had on the other. She considers the question of whether Plath can be considered 'a passive victim' with Hughes as 'a witness in control', which some versions of the Plath story seem to favour, and concludes that the relationship between the two was essentially symbiotic. Both poets had different styles, both also came from different national contexts and traditions but the interaction between them was one of mutuality. Margaret Uroff points out that their poems constantly explore insights shared and read as parts of a continuing debate about the nature of the universe, in which Plath's reservations and Hughes' assertions play against each other.[7]

She also notes the way in which Plath helped Hughes to publish in the early days of their marriage, in particular helping him to acquire an American readership, whilst he then reversed the pattern and was instrumental in editing and publishing her work after her death.

But the two writers had different approaches to poetry. Several years earlier, in the summer of 1951, Sylvia Plath wrote about her own writing and identified one of the features that was to become a hallmark of her poetry.

(110) The wind has blown a warm yellow moon up over the sea; a bulbous moon, which sprouts in the soiled indigo sky, and spills bright winking petals of light on the quivering black water.

(111) I am at my best in illogical, sensuous description. Witness the bit above. The wind could not possibly blow a moon up over the sea. Unconsciously, without words, the moon has been identified in my mind with a balloon, yellow, light, and bobbing about on the wind. The moon, according to my mood, is not slim, virginal and silver, but fat, yellow, fleshy and pregnant... Technically, I suppose the visual appearance and sound of words, taken alone, may be much like the mechanics of music... or the color and texture of a painting. However, uneducated as I am in this field, I can only guess and experiment.[8]

In this prophetic passage, Sylvia Plath examines her own creative process in the making of a poem, and identifies her skill in what she terms 'illogical, sensuous description'. It is this quality that became evermore apparent, particularly in the last poems she wrote, which are full of extraordinarily powerful and striking lines such as

> The streetlight
> Splits through the rat's-tail
> Pods of the laburnum at nine in the morning
> > 'Letters in November', 11 November 1962
>
> The train leaves a line of breath
> > 'Sheep in Fog', 28 January 1963

The air is a mill of hooks
                              'Mystic', 1 February 1963

Echoes travelling
Off from the center like horses
                              'Words', 1 February 1963

Sylvia Plath and Ted Hughes lived in Cambridge until the spring of 1957, when they moved to the United States, spending the summer in Cape Cod and then moving at the start of the academic year to Smith College, where Plath took up her first teaching post. Increasingly, however, the demands of academic life and the need for physical and psychological space in which to write began to clash and finally, in 1958, they decided to risk full-time writing to see if they could survive without teaching. In a letter to Warren of 11 June 1958, Plath describes their decision and explains their reasoning:

> There is something suspect, especially in America, about people who don't have ten-year plans for a career or at least a regular job. We fitted, amusingly enough, into none of the form categories of 'The Young American Couple'...security to us is in ourselves, and no job, not even money, can give us what we have to develop: faith in our work and hard hard work which is Spartan in many ways.

They lived for a year in Boston and in the summer of 1959 travelled across the United States on holiday. In a letter to her mother of 1 August, Plath notes that she has changed her views on asking Ted Hughes to take out American citizenship, something she had previously expressed hopes that he would want to do. When she became pregnant, Hughes was keen to have the baby born in Britain and so in December 1959 they moved back to England. Reading between the lines, one can sense the familiar story of the differing pulls exerted on both of them by their native environments. Their compromise was to engage in a few years of to-ing and fro-ing across the Atlantic and, in a letter to her mother of 28 October, Sylvia Plath notes that she is growing more pleased with the idea of living in England since 'the speed and expense of America is just about 50 years ahead of me'. In the same letter she expresses her hope that Ted will take her on a trip round England, in the same way as she had taken him on a trip round the United States, exchanging images of their respective countries. In her Journal she records 'a sense of joy and eagerness at living in England' because of the positive reception to some of her recent work there. But she also records 'a series of bad, sleepless nights', possibly due to the 'coming unsettling'.

1960–63: THE LAST YEARS

After a short stay in Yorkshire, Ted Hughes and Sylvia Plath moved to London in February 1960 and, just a few days later, she signed the contract for the publication of her first book of poems, *The Colossus*. In the letter to her mother and Warren in which she tells them about this development, she signs herself 'Your new authoress' (11 February 1960). Then, on 1 April her first child, Frieda, was born. In her letter to her mother and Warren written a few hours after the birth, she records her feelings at the time:

> I looked on my stomach and saw Frieda Rebecca, white as flour with the cream that covers new babies, funny little dark squiggles of hair plastered over her head, with big, dark-blue eyes. At 5:45 exactly. The afterbirth came shortly after. Ted was there the whole time, holding my hand, rubbing my back and boiling kettles – a marvellous comfort. I couldn't take my eyes off the baby. The midwife sponged her beside the bed in my big pyrex mixing bowl, wrapped her up well, near a hot water bottle in the crib; she sucked at me a few minutes like a little expert and got a few drops of colostrum and then went to sleep.

In the months following Frieda's birth Sylvia Plath gradually returned to her writing and the letters home trace her phases of activity, periods of stasis and continued discontent with the English weather, a recurring but significant problem. In February 1961 she had a miscarriage and soon after had her appendix out. Her Journal contains a series of notes on her stay in hospital and the minute details noted down about people and objects show the kind of mental processes of observation that are also revealed in the poetry:

> 'The old lady's plastic flesh-coloured neckpiece on her table like an extra head – peach-pink with air holes, white straps and silver studs and a lining of yellow sponge and pink-flowered nightgown silk.'
> *Bed 1*: Joan in a plastercast from toe to bosom for 4 months knits dark green wool. Has a house on the sea in South Devon. Obvious

brave front. Reads *Horse and Hound*. Two sons 16 and 14. Sent to public school at 6. 'The only thing'. Her entomologist husband, their life in Africa, studying locusts.[9]

In 1960 she had begun work on her autobiographical novel, *The Bell Jar*, and by early 1961, when the miscarriage and operation interrupted her, she had written a good part of it. Though the experience of her breakdown and lengthy process of recovery that forms the basis of the novel was some eight years behind her, the spell in hospital must have woken old memories. The images of whiteness, of the self wrapped in mummy-like bandages, of shipwreck, stones and water run through the novel and return in many of the poems that date from the period of her hospitalisation. In 'Tulips', dated 18 March 1961, she writes:

> I have let things slip, a thirty-year-old cargo boat
> Stubbornly hanging onto my name and address.
> They have swabbed me clear of my loving associations

The dead babies of *The Bell Jar*, a recurring motif throughout the novel, mirror in fiction the child lost through miscarriage.

In the summer of 1961, Sylvia Plath was pregnant again and her son Nicholas was born in January 1962. Meanwhile, she and Ted Hughes had decided to move out of London and had bought a thatched cottage in Devon. Her letters home describe her enthusiasm for country life, her attempts to integrate into the local community and her continued pleasure in motherhood. But again the dislike of winter comes through; in a letter to her mother of 5 November she writes:

> The next five months are grim ones. I always feel sorry to have the summertime change, with the dark evenings closing in mid-afternoon, and will try to lay in some physical comforts these months – the best insurance against gloominess for me.

Aurelia Plath records that she visited Sylvia in June 1962 but found great tension between her daughter and Ted Hughes. She, and others, attributed this to Ted Hughes' affair with another woman and Sylvia Plath's inability to cope with it. The tension she was experiencing shows up in the poems dating from this period; in the summer of 1962, poem after poem speaks of anguish at the loss of love:

Who has dismembered us?
The dark is melting.
We touch like cripples.

'Event', 21 May 1961

Sulfurous adulteries grieve in a dream.
Cold glass, how you insert yourself

'The Other', 2 July 1962

Now the room is ahiss. The instrument
Withdraws its tentacle. But the spawn percolate in my heart. They are fertile.

'Words heard, by accident, over the phone', 11 July 1962

I made a fire; being tired
Of the white fists of old
Letters and their death rattle
When I came too close to the wastebasket.

'Burning the Letters', 13 August 1962

What was she doing when it blew in
Over the seven hills, the red furrow, the blue mountain?
Was she arranging cups? It is important.
Was she at the window, listening?
In that valley the train shrieks echo like souls on hooks.

'The Detective', 1 October 1962

In a letter to her mother of 27 August, she tells her that she is going to try for a legal separation from Ted Hughes, adding 'I do not believe in divorce and would never think of this.' Through the autumn, she followed up her decision to see a solicitor and began commuting to London to try to set up work projects that would make her financially independent. All through this time she wrote and in a letter to her mother of 16 October she describes this writing phase:

I am a writer...I am a genius of a writer; I have it in me. I am writing the best poems of my life; they will make my name. I could finish the novel in six *weeks* of day-long work. I have a gift of inspiration for another.

In December she moved into a flat in London with the children. Her novel, published under a pseudonym (Victoria Lucas) appeared in

January 1963. She continued to write a great unstoppable burst of poems day after day but her dread of English winters was made worse by the fact that the winter of 1962–63 was the coldest for more than a century. Still, in her letters home, she struggles to be optimistic, to write hopefully about her future. On 4 February she wrote to her mother:

> I shall simply have to fight it out on my own over here. Maybe someday I can manage holidays in Europe with the children. The children need me most right now, so I shall try to go on for the next few years writing mornings, being with them afternoons and seeing friends or studying and reading evenings.

But on that same day she wrote 'Contusion', a prefiguration of what was to come in the last three lines

> The heart shuts,
> The sea slides back,
> The mirrors are sheeted.

Early on 11 February, before the children woke, she gassed herself. There was a note giving her doctor's telephone number and asking for whoever found it to call him (her baby-sitter was expected at 9 a.m.). The baby-sitter arrived on time but was unable to get into the flat and by the time help had been called and the door was opened Sylvia Plath was dead. Her last poem, written on 5 February, 'Edge' opens with the now famous lines

> The woman is perfected.
> Her dead
> Body wears the smile of accomplishment

The Journal entries from the last months of her life, right up to three days before her death, were destroyed by Ted Hughes. As he explains in his Foreword to the Journal when it was published, he destroyed it because he did not want the children to have to read it and because 'in those days I regarded forgetfulness as an essential part of survival'.

THE SUICIDE

Paramount among the concerns of biographical critics out for the 'truth' about Sylvia Plath is the need to somehow explain her decision to kill herself. Various theories are offered – that she was playing a game with death, gambling with her own life as the stake but assuming that she would, of course, survive, that the suicide was never intended but was an attention-getting device, that it was a momentary aberration in a particularly dark period of her life. None of these attempts to explain away what happened seem worthwhile pursuing; what remains for readers today is the fact that she *did* die and die at her own hand. Nor can that decision which she took on a bitterly cold February morning in 1963 be so surprising. Admittedly, she had her children in the house with her but the emotional and physical pressures on her were such that anyone might understandably crack beneath such a weight. Within barely three years she had left her native United States to live in a country that intrigued her but whose climate eroded her health and sense of well-being, she had given birth to two children and miscarried a third, her adored husband was involved with someone else and she was writing at an exhausting pace, juggling the domestic parts of her life around the flow of creativity that she needed to fulfil. Small wonder that there were times when she felt unable to cope. The simple fact of organising her working and domestic life, always difficult but made doubly so by the need to become the breadwinner once the marriage had failed, was an enormous burden to take on. If we add to that the anguish she must have felt at the death of her one great love, it seems spurious to even question the fact that there must have been times – perhaps many of them – when death must have seemed like the only obvious step to take.

The best-known discussion of Sylvia Plath's death is A. Alvarez's Prologue to his book, *The Savage God*. Alvarez describes how he met Plath in 1960, when he was poetry critic for *The Observer*, and how she shared her poetry with him in the last phase of her writing. His interpretation of her death is that it was both a cry for help that misfired and 'a last desperate attempt to exorcise the death she had summoned up in her poems'.[10] He is sympathetic, struggling to understand how 'such waste', as he terms it, can be explained and whether there is 'a tradition of suicide, . . .' and 'quasi-literary forces' that led her to it. But despite his concern for this 'tradition' of suicide, he seems to miss that aspect of Sylvia Plath's life and work which has been focused upon by other women writers, such as Ann Sexton, which is the kaleidoscopic nature of existence, a life made up of many fragments that defies rational explanation and categorisation. As Ann Sexton says, when she and Sylvia Plath used to meet, they never asked 'Why build?'; they simply asked each other 'Which

tools?' Rejecting all attempts at 'finding out' anything about Plath's
last decision, Ann Sexton says:

> Never mind last diggings. They don't matter. What matters is her
> poems. These last poems stun me. They eat time.[11]

The last poems do show a fascination with death and with pain,
both physical and mental. 'Lady Lazarus', written between 23 and
29 October 1962, contains the famous lines

> Dying
> Is an art, like everything else.
> I do it exceptionally well.

But that same poem also shows another aspect of Plath's writing
about death, the myth of the phoenix, of the rebirth out of suffering.
Significantly, 'Lady Lazarus' ends with a reference to rebirth

> Out of the ash
> I rise with my red hair
> And I eat men like air.

A reading of Plath's poems that hunts for prefigurations of her
suicide is an obviously tempting approach and many critics have
chosen to do just that. But it is nevertheless just one kind of reading
and it is a restricted reading at that. The poems are full of pain, of
references to suffering and death as release from suffering but to
read them as coded references to her suicide seems unfair. Better to
read the poems, as Ann Sexton suggests, for their own sake, for what
they say to those who read them, rather than in an attempt to use
them in the making of the text that is Sylvia Plath's life. All that is
clear in any reading is the fluency of expression and the force of
emotion behind the words on the printed page. What can any reader
conclude from those lines in her last poem, 'Edge', for example,
about dead children:

> Each child coiled, a white serpent,
> One at each little
> Pitcher of milk, now empty.
> She has folded
> Them back into her body as petals

Of a rose close when the garden
Stiffens and odors bleed
From the sweet, deep throats of the nightflower.

Is there, behind these lines, a thought of dying *with* her children, like
Medea, the wronged wife who killed her children before ascending
into the skies in a chariot? She had used the Medea myth before. In
'The Bee Meeting' (3 October 1962), for example, is the line: 'The
upflight of the murderess into a heaven that loves her'. The fourth
line of the poem refers to the 'illusion of a Greek necessity' and the
last line tells us that the moon 'has nothing to be sad about' since she
is used to 'this sort of thing'. It is a possible reading and I for one find
it hard to approach this poem without the Medea legend also in my
mind. But such a reading can no more be argued for as definitive
than that which refutes such a suggestion completely. Nor really
does it matter whether there was ever such a thought behind the
writing of it. In the end, Sylvia Plath chose to kill herself alone. What
we are left with is the pain in the poem and the pain of knowing
that she died.

DEATH IN CONTEXT

Sylvia Plath's poetry, full as it is of references to death, is by no
means focused on her own death. In the poems collected in the
volume *Ariel* and some of the later ones, there are references to different kinds of death, in particular to death in the concentration camps.
Far from becoming more self-absorbed in the last years and months
of her life, Sylvia Plath seems to have been developing a political
consciousness and in her poems and letters there are references to
her fears of nuclear war and her growing interest in politics. In a
letter to her mother of 21 April 1960 she describes how she went on
the Aldermaston Easter Sunday March with Ted Hughes and the
baby in a carrycot:

I saw the first of the 7-mile-long column appear – red and orange
and green banners, 'Ban the Bomb' etc., shining and swaying
slowly. Absolute silence. I found myself weeping to see the tan,
dusty marchers, knapsacks on their backs – Quakers and Catholics,
Africans and whites, Algerians and French – 40 per cent were
London housewives. I felt proud that the baby's first real adventure

should be as a protest against the insanity of world-annihilation. Already a certain percentage of unborn children are doomed by fallout and no one knows the cumulative effects of what is already poisoning the air and sea.

'Fever 103°', dated 20 October 1962, links the horrors of nuclear attack with her anguish at the betrayal of trust in marriage:

> Devilish leopard!
> Radiation turned it white
> And killed it in an hour
> Greasing the bodies of adulterers
> Like Hiroshima ash and eating in.
> The sin. The sin.

One year earlier, in a letter to her mother written in December 1961, she had talked at length about her fears of American armament policies:

> I began to wonder if there was any point in trying to bring up children in such a mad, self-destructive world ... I just wish England had the sense to be neutral, for it is quite obvious that she would be 'obliterated' in any nuclear war, and for this reason I am very much behind the nuclear disarmers here.

The image of the nuclear holocaust, of the ashes and malformed human remains of Hiroshima fuses with the image of the concentration camps in the poems from 1960 onwards. At the same time there is evidence of her will to become involved, to do something to help. In the same letter of 21 April 1960, she urges her mother and brother not to vote for Nixon, and asks for advice as to how she can go about voting in England because 'I never have and feel badly to be deprived of however minute a participation in political affairs.'

Political affairs during Sylvia Plath's lifetime meant something very different than they had meant to previous generations. Born in 1932, she was still a child when the United States joined the Second World War, and an adolescent when that war ended and dreams of a new, Utopian society came into circulation. In the year that she graduated and went on to Smith College those dreams were already a myth of the past. It was in the year 1950 in which Alger Hiss was sent to jail, in which McCarthy alleged that the US State Department employed over 200 Communists, in which Klaus Fuchs was sent to jail in Britain for allegedly selling atomic secrets to the Russians, the year when North Korean forces captured Seoul, and the USSR announced to the world that it too had a nuclear bomb. The early years of the fifties were dominated by the continuance of the Cold War and the growing fears of nuclear conflict. In Britain, food rationing continued until 1954 and there building of the bombed inner cities took much longer than had been anticipated. In the United States anti-Communist paranoia reached epic proportions and the censorship of the media was almost as bad as that imposed under Stalin.

In 1956, the year in which Sylvia Plath met Ted Hughes, a point of crisis was reached. The Hungarian uprising was crushed by Russian tanks and, despite all the anti-Communist rhetoric, the United States did nothing to help. Communist intellectuals throughout Europe left the party in droves, the face of left-wing politics was totally changed. But so also was the face of right-wing politics, for in that same year the British and French invaded Suez in a last-ditch imperialist intervention and the United States again failed to assist. This time, however, the American refusal to intervene behind Britain and France marked the collapse of the British Empire's world status. The balance of power was now firmly held between the United States and the USSR and the days of Britain's greatness were marked as over forever.

1956 was a significant year in which to be living in Britain for other reasons too, for it was in that year that the production of John Osborne's *Look Back in Anger*, followed immediately by Joan Littlewood's Theatre Workshop productions of Brendan Behan's *The Quare Fellow* and Shelagh Delaney's *A Taste of Honey*, changed British theatre and British cultural life generally in an irrevocable way. The new generation of writers and actors came not from the educated middle class but from the educated working class. They brought with them an alternative vision of the British class structure and a sense of anger at the loss of the post-war dreams of a new egalitarian society. With the new theatre came the new wave of novelists, to be followed a short while later by the poets, who perhaps held out the longest against the tide of change. The ground was being laid for the explosion of working-class culture and the left-wing intellectualism of the middle sixties.

In the United States 1956 was perhaps not so significant a year as 1959, for in that year Fidel Castro became leader in Cuba. America's Suez was to be the infamous Bay of Pigs episode in 1963, the new wave of writing in America was shortly to follow along with the Civil Rights Movement and, in the middle sixties also, the growth of the anti-war movement as the United States became more heavily involved in military conflict in Vietnam and southeast Asia. Living in those years, however, as someone who crossed the Atlantic often and had ties in both Britain and the United States, it is impossible to imagine that Sylvia Plath would not have become involved in major social preoccupations.

The generation that came to maturity in the 1950s suffered from the shadow cast by the past, in the form of the Second World War, and the shadow cast by the future menace of nuclear conflict. It was a generation that did not have the clarity of commitment that marked the previous generation which had fought in Spain and in the Second World War, whilst the generation that was to follow, born at the end of that war, did not have the ambiguity that so many people felt in the fifties. The sixties was a decade of greater confidence, a period in which ideals of social harmony were once again possible. Sylvia Plath belonged to the generation caught in between the two – the old and the new hopefulness. Here was the generation that found itself on the edge, between the age of empire and the nuclear age, between austerity and affluence, between elitist cultural ideals and working class, racially integrated ideals. As she asks in the last lines of a poem, *The Babysitter*, dated 29 October 1961:

What keyhole have we slipped through, what door has shut?
The shadows of the grasses inched round like hands of a clock,
And from our opposite continents we wave and call.
Everything has happened.

PLATH'S WRITINGS

Sylvia Plath seems to have set the most store by having her prose works published. She published stories and other short pieces throughout her life and in his preface to *Johnny Panic and the Bible of Dreams* Ted Hughes quotes her statement that poetry was an 'evasion from the real job of writing prose'. Discussing her ambition to write stories, he notes that 'successful story-writing, for her, had all the advantages of a top job' since she wanted both the money and the status. But he also describes her fears of inadequacy in this her chosen career and her growing frustration as she began to discover that she could write poetry with greater fluency than she could prose:

> She couldn't understand why it was so difficult for her, when other writers seemed to find it so easy, and when even she had found it fairly easy in the past, during her teens. How had it become such an impossibly stubborn language for her, and why was the whole effort loaded with such terrors?

Ted Hughes' brief account of her writing practice ties in with her account of her problems in the Journal. She went through the great barrier of 'shouldism', of feeling that she ought to write in a certain way, that life and art should somehow be kept apart from one another, that her 'life' should not intrude into her writing. Once through that barrier, she could find her own writing voice and the difference between that voice and the slightly contrived writing of much of her short prose is clearly heard. Hughes implies that his view is that her best stories are those 'where her own natural voice begins to come through', that is, where she abandoned the search for a favourable judgement from an imaginary readership and wrote out of experience. Certainly, the feeling in the poems is very much that of an authentic voice; not because she wrote *about* her life in the narrow sense, certainly not because she structured her experience, but because she was writing *within* her life, as part of it. The kind of writing process that involved the structuring of (often painful) experiences seems in her case to have resulted in greater power and intensity. At least, the reading of her works by this reader has led to that conclusion.

In her lifetime, she published stories in a variety of magazines, both in the United States and in Britain. Most of the surviving stories are collected together in the *Johnny Panic* volume which was published in 1977. Of her other prose, her notebooks and an abridged version of the Journal were collated and published as *The Journals of Sylvia Plath* in 1982. The unabridged version, edited by Karen V. Kukil came out in 2000. Her novel, *The Bell Jar*, was published shortly before she died in 1963 under a pseudonym and, as Mary Kinzie notes, the few reviews that appeared were 'illiterate'.[12] Most reviewers did not know that the novel was by Sylvia Plath and it failed to attract much attention until after her death, when it was reprinted in 1967 under her own name. A second novel, with the working title of

Double Exposure, disappeared. Ted Hughes says that about 130 pages of it had been written at the time of her death.

Her first collection of poems, *The Colossus*, came out in 1960. *Ariel*, a second collection that she had been preparing before she died, came out in 1965. Also in 1965, Turret Press issued a volume entitled *Uncollected Poems*. *Crossing the Water*, containing most of the poems written between the two previous collections, appeared in 1971 and in that same year *Winter Trees* also appeared, a volume containing some of the last poems and her 1962 verse play for radio, *Three Women*. Ted Hughes' edition of her collected poems, which includes the four collections and some of her juvenilia, was published in 1981 and won the Pulitzer Prize.

Today the reader has access to her poems, different versions of her Journals, her novel, her short prose, her letters – all the printed texts of her life's work. The reader also has access to the steady stream of books and articles about her life and work and, of course, to the works of Ted Hughes who, some years after his wife's death, joined the long line of Poets Laureate.

2
Poetry as Process

The first edition of Sylvia Plath's Journals edited by Ted Hughes and Frances MacCullagh, was published in 1982, one year after the appearance of her *Collected Poems*. Eighteen years later, in 2000, Karen V. Kukil edited a full, unabridged version of the Journals, using the 23 extant handwritten and typed manuscripts that span Plath's adult life, from her years as a student at Smith College to the period shortly before her death. The Journals shed light not only on Plath's thoughts about writing, but also on her creative process. They are clearly personal documents about her feelings, but were also a space in which she could try out ideas and note incidents and thoughts that she would later transform through language, either in her prose writing or in her poetry.

Though intensely personal, the Journals are on one level consistent: even when written in haste, there is a strong sense of style and a powerful literary quality. Sylvia Plath analysed endlessly not only her own personal feelings, particularly about love and sex but also what it meant for her to be a writer. In an entry for 12 December 1958 she defines writing as follows:

> Writing is a religious act: it is an ordering, a reforming, a relearning and reloving of people and the world as they are and as they might be. A shaping which does not pass away like a day of typing or a day of teaching. The writing lasts: it goes about on its own in the world ... You do it for itself first. If it brings in money, how nice. You do not do it first for money ... The worst thing would be to live with not writing.[1]

Yet a few lines before this almost metaphysical statement Sylvia Plath wrote that she wanted to 'write stories and poems and a novel and be Ted's wife and a mother'. Important though the writing was to her, being a wife and mother is ranked on the same level. Her life can be seen as a balancing act, trying to sustain with equal success what she saw as her vocation as a creative artist alongside her vocation as wife and mother. There is an intensely practical side to Sylvia Plath that comes across from the Journals, and coexists with her expressions of a more abstract, spiritual nature. The myth of the writer and the desire to live that myth was one that she expressed powerfully, but at the same time she recorded her interest in practical details and her fascination for the particular. The Journals show also that she was constantly testing her skills as a prose writer, including long passages of detailed description and dialogues, creating portraits of individual characters, in short transforming her everyday experiences into a form of fiction. Here, for example, is Plath writing about a banal incident in a parking lot in February, 1958:

> Just as I drove into the snow-piled parking lot behind the first National & got out to stride to the back door, hands bare & tucked futilely into my coat sleeves, coat blowing open & wind on my bare throat, the heavy metal apparatus of the swinging door hinge came loose & hit a woman on the head: she stood, singled out in a muddy maroon coloured coat, ugly, violated: 'It struck my head', and as I pushed into the store, past starers, a nasty, mean mealy mouthed man, chest stuck out under a blue monogrammed jacket & a face blotched & pale as bad sausage, came pushing out to repair, to right, to make amends.[2]

In this extract, Plath turns an ordinary incident in a parking lot into something vaguely sinister; the characters are unpleasant, their movements and clothing contrast with her own free stride and openness suggested in her account of her clothes (coat blowing open, wind on her bare throat). Plath, the heroine, is surrounded by squalor, by small, mean, ugly people. This sense of her own separateness, of being somehow set apart from other mortals runs through her Journals. For Plath, being a writer meant being different, for the craft of the writer went together with a sense of vocation, a sense of being driven by writing. Years later, in 'Kindness' she would write

> The blood jet is poetry
> There is no stopping it.

Also in the Journals are passages of minutely detailed description, not only of people and places but also of things. Among the fragments included in Appendix 11 to the volume are a series of still-life pictures in words of pine cones, corn vases and a trailer, presumably written as exercises or as notes to be used at some later date. The detail with which she looked at objects is exemplified in the following extract:

> Turning the pine cone in the hand and regarding it in profile, one sees the tiny upper petals point skyward, gradually level out horizontal half way down, dark at the central stem and tipped with a whitish crescent, like a shallow saucer with a thorn-point base, and then, the lowest petals turn downward, spaced in a row, and the next row staggered beneath to form a fairly solid base of wooden frills.[3]

This kind of attention to detail can be seen again and again in her poetry. Here, in 'Resolve' written in 1956, the poem zooms in onto small, in themselves insignificant images, which disquietingly accentuate the overall mood of anxiety:

> outside, the little hedge leaves
> are become quite yellow
> a milk-film
> blurs
> the empty bottles on the windowsill
> no glory descends
>
> two water drops poise
> on the arched green
> stem of my neighbor's rose bush

The sense of anxiety is created by the cumulative effect of the little leaves that have become yellow, the film that blurs the empty bottles, the water drops about to fall. Plants and inanimate objects are in a state of suspense on a day described in the opening line as 'a day of mist'. The clue to the sense of anxiety comes at the end of the poem, with a reference to 'twelve black-gowned examiners' and the speaker's fears of failure, encapsulated in the last lines:

> today I will not
> disenchant my twelve black-gowned examiners
> or bunch my fist
> in the wind's sneer.

Photographic detail is used differently in 'Medallion' (1959), where a dead snake is described as being 'inert as a shoelace'. The speaker of the poem picks up the snake, turns it around in her hand, noting the changing colours of the skin on the snake's belly, its tongue 'a rose-coloured arrow', the maggots 'thin as pins in the dark bruise'. The dead snake is beautiful, its scales like chain mail studded with jewels. In this poem, the language transforms the snake into a mythical creature, its death a heroic defeat at the hands of an unworthy adversary:

> Knifelike, he was chaste enough
> Pure death's-metal. The yardman's
> Flung brick perfected his laugh.

Plath's conscious focussing on minute detail is almost cinematic, as the eye of the poet functions like a camera. At the same time, the skilful use of words, particularly adjectives and verbs endows the scene with significance. 'Poppies in July' (20 July 1962) offers a personification of the flowers through the same zoom-lens technique of attention to tiny detail. The poppies are described in the first line as 'little hell flames', though theirs is a cold fire that does not burn:

> Flickering like that, wrinkly and clear red, like the skin of a mouth
> A mouth just bloodied
> Little bloody skirts!

The flickering of the petals can seem like flames, but also wrinkled like the skin of a mouth. No sooner has the image of the mouth been introduced than another level of violence emerges. The mouth is bloodied, and the next line reinforces the idea that the victim of that violence is a woman: the poppy petals are 'little bloody skirts'. The sight of poppies in a field in July is transformed into a string of sinister images that hint at domestic violence and pain, made almost explicit with the two lines that start with the conditional 'if':

> If I could bleed, or sleep!
> . . . .
> If my mouth could marry a hurt like that!

Plath's technique of zooming in on a small image from everyday reality, then expanding it outwards to acquire new layers of meaning is one that is repeated over and over in her poetry. The beginnings of that technique can be seen early on in the Journals, becoming more apparent later when she had begin to write more poetry and to experiment with form and language.

Part of the writer's duty, as Sylvia Plath saw it, was to record and to remember, hence the Journals illustrate her recording process. Some of the entries stand almost as entities in their own right, whilst others are merely sketches. Reading the Journals, it is important to remember that they were not intended to be read by anyone else, so the process of self-representation functioned more like a mirror than as a self-advertisement. The young woman who aspired to greatness as a writer recorded her struggles along the path to that greatness, and recorded in parallel her doubts and anxieties, her love affairs, her complex relationships with family and friends and her passionate interest in the minutiae of the world she lived in.

Particularly interesting are those points in the Journals where incidents or scenes recorded reappear later in poems, for here the transformative processes are seen most clearly. One such example is the entry for 7 June 1962. Sylvia Plath gives this entry a title, 'CHARLIE POLLARD & The Beekeepers' and it clearly served as an aid to her when writing her bee poems, most especially 'The Bee Meeting'. The Journal entry records how she and Ted rushed down to the local Devonshire beekeepers' meeting as they were interested in starting a hive of their own. The meeting is recorded in detail, with portraits of the various characters including Charlie Pollard, the rector and a midwife. Plath relates how she was given protective clothing, since she had no hat or coat, she describes the allotment gardens they walked through to reach the hives, then her first experience of coming close to bees. The entry for 8 June records how she and Ted drove over to Charlie Pollard's house to collect their hive.

Bees, as many biographers have pointed out, were significant in a special way to Sylvia Plath, since her father had been an expert on bees and had written research papers and a monograph. In her Journals she describes the meeting with the beekeepers in her usual clear prose, with a slight hint of humour as can be seen in this passage:

Then the rector came pontificating across the bridge & there was a silence that grew round him. He carried a curious contraption ...a dark felt hat with a screen box built on under it, and cloth for a neckpiece under that. I thought the hat a clerical bee-keeping hat, and that he must have made it for himself. Then I saw, on the grass, and in hands, everybody was holding a bee-hat, some with netting of nylon, most with box screening, some with khaki round

hats, I felt barer & barer. People became concerned. Have you no
hat? Have you no coat? Then a dry little woman came up, Mrs
Jenkins, the secretary of the society, with tired, short blond hair.
'I have a boilersuit.' She went to her car and came back with a small,
white silk button-down smock, the sort pharmacist's assistants
use. I put it on and buttoned it & felt more protected.[4]

In 'The Bee Meeting', this encounter between the prospective
beekeepers and the experts related in gently comic terms as an
encounter with the peculiar inhabitants of a Devonshire village is
transformed into something completely different. The bee poems
are a powerful cluster of five poems included in *Ariel* that have been
read in different ways. Susan R. Van Dyne, for example, in a book
that is based on a close examination of Sylvia Plath's drafts and the
revisions she made to those drafts, sees the poems as moving from
a state of passivity to one of hope.[5] She also points out that Sylvia Plath
ordered her version of *Ariel* in such a way that it concluded with the
bee poems. This would have meant that *Ariel* opened with the word
'Love' and ended with the last word of 'Wintering' which is 'spring'.
When Ted Hughes edited the volume for his dead wife, he chose
instead to conclude with a different poem, 'Words', so that the last
word of *Ariel* is 'life'. Either way, both Sylvia Plath and Ted Hughes
clearly intended the collection to conclude on a note of affirmation.

'The Bee Meeting' recounts the episode recorded in the Journals
in totally different terms, as the first two verses indicate:

Who are these people at the bridge to meet me? They are the villagers –
The rector, the midwife, the sexton, the agent for bees.
In my sleeveless summery dress I have no protection,
And they are all gloved and covered, why did nobody tell me?
They are smiling and taking out veils tacked to ancient hats.

I am nude as a chicken neck, does nobody love me?
Yes, here is the secretary of bees with her white shop smock,
Buttoning the cuffs at my wrists and the slit from my neck to my
knees.
Now I am milkweed silk, the bees will not notice.
They will not smell my fear, my fear, my fear.

In this poem the poet has become a sacrificial victim, the borrowing
of a smock becomes part of a ritual in which it appears that she is

being prepared for sacrifice. The villagers appear part of a grotesque ceremony that the speaker of the poem cannot understand. The poem is structured around a series of questions that cannot be answered, and words like *slit*, *knotted*, *blood clots*, *surgeon*, *butcher*, *armoury*, *spiky*, *hunting* run through the first nine verses hinting at something terrible which is articulated in verse 10, when the queen bee flies, a Medea figure:

> The upflight of the murderess into a heaven that loves her

The final verse, after the flight of the queen sees the end of the ritual, as the villagers untie their disguises. The I-speaker claims to be 'exhausted' and the poem ends on a question

> Whose is that long white box in the grove, what have they accomplished, why am I cold.

Written in October 1962, just a few months after the June entry in the Journal, 'The Bee Meeting' offers a good example of the way in which Sylvia Plath was able to transform the everyday into the extraordinary, and through a process of mythologisation to create a complex ritualised depiction of her anger and distress, using the images and even much of the language of her earlier piece of writing. The difference between the account of her meeting with the Devonshire beekeepers in her Journal and the sequence of bee poems is immense.

There can be no simple, definitive reading of Sylvia Plath's poetry or of her life. Only by accepting that contradictions exist in a dialectical relationship with each other can we move beyond a dead-end 'reading to find out the truth' kind of process. Information of various kinds about Sylvia Plath is available, her poems and stories, letters and articles are on library shelves, people who knew her (and some people who did not) have offered their own subjective comments. But beyond this evidence there can be nothing more. Sylvia Plath's own texts offer contradictions that sometimes appear to be unbelievably extreme. She was capable of huge swings of mood, and her writing shows this clearly. Moreover, as a writer she transformed experience into something else, moving away from the ordinary onto a different plane. She deliberately wrote in the first person, not so much out of any conscious desire to write her own autobiography, but in order to try out different voices. She makes this explicit in the Journal when she says

My one salvation is to enter into other characters in stories: the only three stories I am prepared to see published are all told in the first person. The thing is, to develop other first persons.[6]

It is worth bearing in mind two simple points when approaching a writer like Sylvia Plath. The first is to recognise the impossibility of consistency. No-one who has ever been through any kind of personal crisis (and there can be few people who have not) can have failed to note the great swings of mood that are part of heightened emotional living. It is possible to be darkly depressed on a Monday, full of energy on a Tuesday, weepy on Wednesday, the life and soul of the party on Thursday and during that time to write letters or to make telephone calls alternating between the desperate and the jovial. And since this is a normal human state of being, why should we demand consistency from a writer who left us a record in print of some of those shifts of mood? It is impossible to try to discover the 'real' Sylvia Plath, to work out the 'real' reason for her suicide, because there is no 'real' person and no 'real' explanation. Sylvia Plath, like the rest of us, was a complex human being full of contradictory impulses and feelings and, perhaps more honestly than many of us, she recorded those contradictions in her work. 'Oh heart, such disorganisation!' she says in 'Appearance', a poem written in 1962. The disorganised heart, which we accept in ourselves, seems to be something that the dead are not allowed to have had, fixed as they become in the processes of concretisation that go on afterwards.

The second point arises out of the first. Just as it is impossible to discover the 'truth' about anyone else's heart, so it is impossible to have a single true reading of a work. We have come to recognise that there is no such thing as a single definitive reading of anything, that there are as many versions of a text as there are readers reading it and though there have been some attempts to restrict the anarchy of that suggestion we are today offered the prospect of a text as an open entity. And that openness is particularly evident in poetry, even more so in a poetry as imagistic as Sylvia Plath's, for each rereading of her poems uncovers layers of significance that each reader constructs for him or herself. In 'Poppies in October', when the poet writes:

> Oh my God, what am I
> That these late mouths should cry open
> In a forest of frost, in a dawn of cornflowers.

The *I* that is Sylvia Plath writing dissolves into the *I* of each of us reading, and we bring our own subjective responses to those lines. The poem, once written, is rewritten in every reading and the notion of a single definitive reading becomes the absurdity it is. The power of her writing, combined with the power of the reader's rewriting cannot fail to transform. In 'Words' Sylvia Plath offers the image of words like riderless horses and writes of the transforming power of words:

> Axes
> After whose stroke the wood rings,
> And the echoes!
> Echoes travelling
> Off from the center like horses.

In an essay entitled 'The Poetry of Sylvia Plath: A Technical Analysis', John Fredrick Nims argues that Plath produced poetry of 'timeless excellence', since she had such a strong sense of language and metaphor and was aware of the physical rhythms of her verse. Perhaps surprisingly, he singles out her early work *The Colossus* for special praise, suggesting that in this collection we can clearly see Plath's craftsmanship as she worked on her poetry, and experimented in different ways:

> I might begin by saying to young writers: forget *Ariel* for a while; study *The Colossus*. Notice all the stanza forms, all the uses of rhythm and rhyme; notice how the images are chosen and related; how deliberately sound is used.... Perhaps for writers this is the gist of the Plath case: without the drudgery of *The Colossus*, the triumph of *Ariel* is unthinkable.[7]

Nims sees *The Colossus* as a series of exercises, almost an apprenticeship collection and examines the way in which Plath played with rhyme, drawing upon her extensive reading of earlier poets and refining her verse in ways that would enable her to write more freely later. He notes the patterns of repetition, the brilliant use of metaphor, the games Plath played with stress patterns and rhymes. Central to his argument are Plath's own words about her writing, the statements she made that were recorded in 1962 about the importance of the poet being able to control and structure experiences, 'even the most terrifying, like madness...and should be able to manipulate those experiences with an informed and intelligent mind.'[8]

Far from seeking to conceal Plath's poetry, or to diminish her achievement, Ted Hughes has consistently presented her writings to the world with great professionalism and care. He edited her manuscripts, and in 1981 produced a volume of her *Collected Poems*, which usefully has dates added so that the poems can be read in chronological sequence. Hughes' introduction to the collection is also one of the most valuable accounts of how she wrote, how she organised her thoughts and sought to shape her material.

> Her attitude to her verse was artisan-like: if she couldn't get a tale out of the material, she was quite happy to get a chair, or even a toy.[9]

This important statement depicts Plath as a writer who saw words as a raw material to be shaped into a final product, just as the woodcarver takes a piece of wood and tries to make it into something, no matter how small, letting the material dictate the final shape. Hughes points out that she meticulously dated all her drafts, and uses a beautiful natural image to describe the stages of her poetic development:

> Her evolution as a poet went rapidly through successive moults of style, as she realised her true manner and voice. Each fresh phase tended to bring out a group of poems bearing a general family likeness, and is usually associated in my memory with a particular time and place. At each move we made, she seemed to shed a style.[10]

Hughes singles out one period in the years he and Plath shared as most significant for her poetry. A year after their marriage, Hughes and Plath travelled to the United States, and in the summer of 1959 they drove across the country, through Wisconsin and the Dakotas, down from Montana to Colorado, across the Rockies to California, then eastwards again, across the Mojave desert, through Arizona and the Grand Canyon, to New Orleans and back north to Boston. The journey inspired several poems, but it was not until the autumn, when Hughes and Plath were staying at the writers' and artists' centre in Yaddo, in Upper New York State that Plath's poetic breakthrough happened. She was pregnant by then, prey to mixed emotions after the rejection of her first poetry collection and facing perhaps for the first time the implications of her American and English existences. Hughes dwells on the Yaddo period in his Introduction, noting how she decided to start writing a new collection:

This decision to start a new book 'regardless', and get rid of all that she'd written up to then, coincided with the first real breakthrough in her writing, as it is now possible to see. The actual inner process of this quite sudden development is interestingly recorded, in a metaphorical way, in 'Poem for a Birthday', which she was thinking about on 22 October 1959.[11]

Significantly, Hughes' final collection of poems in which he broke his silence about his feelings towards his dead wife, is entitled *Birthday Letters*, and will be discussed more fully in the last chapter. Already, though, in his Introduction to Plath's *Collected Poems*, Hughes was pointing to 'Poem for a Birthday' as a turning point in Plath's development as a poet.

The label of 'confessional poet' has often been applied to Plath's writing, and certainly she was impressed both by Ann Sexton and by the grand old man of confessional poetry, Robert Lowell. In her Journal entry for 20 March 1959, she notes that in one of Lowell's seminars on criticism of rhetoric, four of her poems were discussed:

He sets me up with Ann Sexton, an honor, I suppose. Well, about time. She has very good things, and they get better, though there is a lot of loose stuff.[12]

Plath did not want 'loose stuff' in her own writing, and in this respect her poetry is different from much confessional poetry, with its stream-of-consciousness flow. Hughes' insistence on the artisan-like quality of Plath's poetry is reflected in the few statements we have made by Plath herself about her writing. In the 1962 interview, Plath insists on the importance of the writer's control of her material, but points out that the individual's pain needs to be related to the broader world-picture:

I think that personal experience is very important, but certainly it shouldn't be a kind of shut-box and mirror-looking, narcissistic experience. I believe it should be relevant to the larger things, the bigger things such as Hiroshima and Dachau and so on.[13]

'Poem for a Birthday' exemplifies Plath's method of fusing intense personal experience with 'bigger things'. The poem is a sequence of seven sections, 'Who; Dark House; Maenad; Flute Notes from a Reedy Pond; Witch Burning; The Stones'. 'Who' opens with a precise location

in time: 'The month of flowering's finished' and is full of autumnal
images. The pumpkins and fading flowers are like mouldering heads,
eyeless but with great gaping mouths. 'I am a root, a stone, an owl
pellet', the poet writes, 'without dreams of any sort.' Blackberry stems
'light me up like an electric bulb', an image that recalls the electric
shock treatment Plath received in hospital. In this autumnal world
of silence and decay, memory fades into nothingness.

The second poem moves from plant to animal imagery. The poet's
pregnancy is represented in animal terms – 'I am as round as an
owl', 'Any day I may litter puppies/Or mother a horse'. In this animal
world, things move underground, in molely tunnels and turnipy
chambers. The third poem, 'Maenad' emerges from the bowels of the
earth into a landscape in which the poet is asserting herself. 'Once
I was ordinary' is the opening line, but by the end of the third verse
Plath writes prophetically 'I am becoming another' and by the last
line she is demanding that the gods respond to her request: 'Tell me
my name.'

The fourth poem, 'The Beast' depicts a bestial husband, a figure
who blows kisses to the bride who 'hardly knew him'. The gap
between husband and wife is expressed through a string of negative
images of refuse and ugliness – 'I've married a cupboard of rubbish...
I bed in a fish puddle...I housekeep in Time's gut-end...Duchess
of Nothing,/Hairtusk's bride.' From this wasteland, the fifth poem
opens with the oncoming cold of winter, the dying colours, the onset
of hibernation. Christ's crucifixion is suggested in the final verse:

> The molts are tongueless that sang from above the water
> Of Golgotha at the tip of a reed

In the sixth poem, it is not crucifixion but the burning of a witch that
provides the central theme, though the final lines are a rejection of
passive suffering and victimhood. 'Give me back my shape' the poet
demands and instead of the torment of flames writhing round a
human body, the poet is filled with light and brightness:

> My ankles brighten. Brightness ascends my thighs.
> I am lost, I am lost, in the robes of all this light.

The profound ambiguity of the imagery of the whole sequence of
poems reaches its climax in the seventh and final poem. The journey
from the eyeless world of autumnal cellars through the sacrificial

moment is over. 'This is the city where men are mended' is the opening line, followed by the sacrificial victim's realisation that she is in another dimension: 'I lie on a great anvil'. 'This is the after-hell... this is the city of spare parts'. Nurses and doctors, stonemasons, workmen, children and mothers employ food tubes, electric currents, catgut stitches, swaddling clothes, hammers, pincers, sponges and chisels as they seek to repair the figure who has fallen out of the light. The last lines offer an image of hope for a future in which the poet is remade:

> Love is the bone and sinew of my curse.
> The vase, reconstructed, houses
> The elusive rose.
> Ten fingers shape a bowl for shadows.
> My mendings itch. There is nothing to do.
> I shall be as good as new.

These lines prefigure the best of the *Ariel* poems. They are rich and dense with images, often loosely connected though always sharp and focussed. The whole sequence can be compared to Dante's *Divine Comedy* in miniature, which also describes the stages of a journey from abandonment, down into the depths of hell and gradually upwards towards enlightenment. In Plath's case, the end is not so much spiritual enlightenment as recognition of who she is: the troubled daughter who is about to become a mother in her own right, the poet struggling to find a voice of her own while married to a man whose reputation as a poet was already established. This recognition process comes about through great suffering, but by the end of the poem it has already started. Hughes is right to single out this sequence as marking a new stage of Plath's creativity.

Margaret Uroff, like a number of subsequent writers, chooses to consider the development of Plath as a poet alongside that of Ted Hughes, arguing that since the two writers lived together during their most formative years it is important to consider the influence each brought to bear upon the other. Uroff also argues that this approach shifts the balance away from readings of Plath as a pathological case study, since many of the aspects of her work that have been seen as emanating from her mental disturbance have parallels in Hughes' writing. Though both writers chose different themes, Uroff notes the shared reading they undertook and proposes that some of the superficial differences between the two poets may be less obvious when we look more deeply. Plath, she points out, appears more interested in psychological states whilst Hughes, at least in his early poetry, writes about the non-human world. Nevertheless, these apparently different interests can be perceived in another way:

> Yet, what is Hughes' interest in animals but an attempt to express the submerged life in himself? And what is Plath's probing of the psyche but a search for the instinctual and elemental qualities of her nature?[14]

From Plath's Journals there is ample evidence of the intensive reading that she and Hughes undertook together, and the closeness of their literary relationship. Plath typed Hughes' manuscripts for him, they read together, exchanged poems, commented on one another's writing, made suggestions, discussed other poets' work. The ongoing dialogue between them has been overlooked in the endeavours to try and arrive at a 'definitive' version of the Plath story and during the years of the demonisation of Hughes, any attempt to show that he might have both influenced and been influenced by his wife would have been received with little sympathy by many readers. Since the publication of *Birthday Letters* in 1998 any doubts about the intensity of their relationship in terms of its mutual benefit artistically can be laid to rest, but the signs were always there for anyone who took the trouble to interpret them.

In a collection of essays on Sylvia Plath that came out in 1985, Ted Hughes published the original extended version of the Introduction he had written for the first edition of the Journals. The essay is both a defence of the decision to publish and a detailed account of Plath's development as a poet as reflected in her notes and Journals. Hughes says that Plath's poetry can be seen as a process of building up to *Ariel*, it is the 'biology of Ariel, the ontology of Ariel – the story of Ariel's imprisonment in the pine before Prospero opened it'.[15] This is a compelling image: Ariel, the spirit that Prospero frees in Shakespeare's *The Tempest*, is a mercurial creature whose great lightness of being disguises a stratum of suffering that was laid down long before Prospero arrived on the island. In a similar way, Hughes suggests that Plath was motivated to write by 'a deep and inclusive inner crisis' that was already formulated in terms of its principal symbols long before she reached maturity. The poems therefore are the expression of the inner working out of that crisis, which he perceives as similar to a biological process. He again insists on the importance of 'Poem for a Birthday', with its final images of rebirth and renewal. The liberation of *Ariel* came with the final poem in the birthday sequence, and from this point onwards, Plath's fluency as a poet could only increase. Hughes sees her as having acquired 'a new position of strength', and praises the poetry she now began to write. The poems that she wrote in April 1962, which include *Crossing the Water* and *Among the Narcissi* are, in his opinion, unique in their calm and poise. On 19 April she wrote *Elm*, and Hughes notes that the manuscript version of this poem shows the poet struggling with her material, battling for control

> when suddenly it burst all her restraints and she let it go. And at once the *Ariel* voice emerged in full. From that day on, it never really faltered again. During the next five months she produced ten more poems. The subject matter didn't alarm her. Why should it, when Ariel was doing the very thing it had been created and liberated to do. In each poem, the terror is encountered head on, and the angel is mastered and brought to terms.[16]

Today, the best-known collection of Plath's poetry is *Ariel*. The 40 poems included in the volume include the most frequently cited and most powerful pieces of her entire output. Though she had begun to organise the collection, it was Hughes who edited the final manuscript and saw it into print in 1965, two years after her death. Hughes admits that he shaped the final version of the manuscript, and also that he included poems written at different times. The earliest, 'You're', was written early in 1960 the latest, 'Edge', was written in February 1963, a few days before her death. In his introduction to the *Collected Poems*, Hughes explains that the final version of *Ariel* was a compromise between publishing a shorter volume, consisting of the twenty or so violent and powerful poems written just before her death and a much longer collection. His intention was to publish a volume that showed the enormous range of Plath's poetic ability, rather than a collection of poems filled with hatred and contradiction. So poems like 'Lesbos' or 'Stopped Dead' written in October 1962 are not included, though 'Fever 103°' written a day later is included. Comparing these three poems, the two which Hughes omitted are far less successful than 'Fever 103°', and show signs of having been written in haste and unrevised. Knowing Plath's attention to detail and contempt for poetry that has not been adequately crafted, Hughes' choice of poems for inclusion in *Ariel* shows meticulous care and respect for his dead wife's art.

The structure of *Ariel* is not chronological, even though 'Morning Song', the opening poem, was written two years before the final rush of violent poems culminating in 'Edge'. The volume opens with a poem about birth, motherhood and love, and ends with a poem about writing, 'Words'. Through *Ariel* we see several different aspects of Plath's writing, and the arrangement of poems foregrounds the differences and shows the range of her technical ability. Despite the way in which some critics have singled out poems like 'Lady Lazarus', 'Daddy', 'Death and Co.' or 'The Applicant' as the most prominent poems in the collection, this is a distorted perspective. They may be among the most shocking in their violence, but they need to be set against some of the more introspective poems and the beautifully crafted series of bee poems which are included as a sequence.

Ariel is a showcase for Plath's poetic talent. After 'Morning Song' come two short poems of great power, constructed as strings of images, 'The Couriers' and 'Sheep in Fog'. These two poems, written at different times late in 1962 are hauntingly beautiful. Lines like 'My bones hold a stillness, the far/Fields melt my heart' ('Sheep in Fog'), 'A ring of gold with the sun in it?/Lies. Lies and a grief' ('The Couriers') are contrasted with the aggressive language of the next poems, 'The Applicant' and 'Lady Lazarus', poems filled with images of the hatefulness of marriage and the powerlessness of women caught in the marriage trap.

Throughout *Ariel* poems of great violence, aggressive poems like 'Getting There', 'Daddy' or 'Cut' are juxtaposed with poems of introspection. 'Elm', for example, returns to Plath's favourite images of trees at night, the sea and the cold whiteness of the moon. The violence of 'Medusa' is followed by a poem from an earlier period, written in October 1961, 'The Moon and the Yew Tree'. The terrifying 'Daddy' is followed by a poem that is almost comic in tone, 'You're' that depicts Plath's unborn child through a string of very physical images

> Our travelled prawn,
> Snug as a bud and at home
> Like a sprat in a pickle jug.
> A creel of eels, all ripples.
> Jumpy as a Mexican bean.

Ariel is a collection of poems that display not only Plath's virtuoso brilliance as a poet, but which can be read as an exposition of her personal mythology. The poems resonate with meaning, referring not only to incidents in her biography, to her parents, her marriage, her children and her despair, but also to those myths and images that she wove into all her writing – the Moon goddess, the quest or journey, the movement from conception to death that is existence, the foetus and the skull, the joy of motherhood and the horror of war.

In his short memoir of Hughes and Plath, Lucas Myers, a close friend from Cambridge writes with great perception about the *Ariel* poems:

> The way the poems of *Ariel* actually function for most people is as a licence for regression or aggression; they function not by way of explaining what is wrong with desires for personal and cultural regression but as a licence granted by virtue of the poetic force, the absoluteness, the power with which they express those desires. The fame of the *Ariel* poems springs not only from the distinction of the verse but from the strategies of the ego that allow the reader confidently to enter into their inward regard with the verse as vehicle.[17]

Sylvia Plath's poetry has been variously termed confessional, symbolist even surrealist as critics have sought to find a suitable term to describe her highly original poetic voice. Great claims have been made for the transformative power of her poetry, but often the generalisations about her collapse when the full range of her writing is considered. It makes most sense to consider her poetry as part of a continuous opus, as Hughes suggests, an ongoing work that, like her Journal, recorded the endless variations in her mood and thought patterns. She comes close at times to confessional poetry, but poems like 'Child', with its images of love and innocence, or 'Gigolo', one of Plath's dramatic monologue poems spoken by a distinctive character do not fit this description. Nor can she be aptly termed a surrealist, for though she uses images in remarkably original ways, those images make sense in terms of her personal cosmography and the germination of many of the images is often discernible in her other writings. In her later period, many of the poems show a strong dramatic flair as Plath tried out different voices, and it is interesting to speculate on whether she might have written more for the theatre or for performance had she lived.

Attempts to pigeonhole Plath in poetic terms run parallel to the attempts to find an answer to the many questions raised by her life and work that have so bedevilled the readers. An alternative to this process of pigeonholing is the reading offered in this book, where Sylvia Plath becomes an example of someone who tried with all her strength to find a way forward in a situation of despair, to cope with pain caused by all kinds of aspects of her life and character and whose death was not because she desired to die but rather because she could not momentarily cope with the anguish of living a life that fell far short of the life she wanted so much to have.

'A Birthday Present', placed halfway through *Ariel* tells us a great deal about the maelstrom of feelings, ideas and images that underpin Plath's poetry. This poem is dated 30 September 1962, a day or so before the sequence of bee poems. Plath had just split up with Hughes and in a letter to her mother of 12 October she writes about how she was getting up at 5 a.m. every day, once the effect of her sleeping pills had worn off, 'writing like mad'. In this period of great personal unhappiness, her writing flourished. Birthdays were important to her as symbolic dates, and in writing a poem about her forthcoming birthday, an important one because she was going to be 30, Plath drew upon everything that had happened in her life, so that the poem can almost be read as a microcosm of all her other poems.

The poem opens with a question: 'What is this, behind this veil, is it ugly, is it beautiful?' The image of the veil being lifted or torn away runs through the poem, used in all kinds of ways. There is the meta-physical veil of the Virgin Mary, that figure who recurs in her poetry time and again in relation to her own mother, then there are the domestic veils – 'the diaphanous satins' of the frost patterns on the windows in January, the whiteness of the drapes around her babies' cots. On another level, veils are seen as cruel, there are veils that suffocate and repress:

> If you only knew how the veils were killing my days.
> To you they are only transparencies, clear air.

In the last lines of the poem she calls for a veil to be let down, another kind of veil, one that will be transformative. This veil is not death, though death-like, for as the knife pierces her side it slides in cleanly and releases the whole universe from within her:

> Only let down the veil, the veil, the veil.
> If it were death

I would admire the deep gravity of it, its timeless eyes.
I would know you were serious.
There would be a nobility then, there would be a birthday.
And the knife not carve, but enter
Pure and clean as the cry of a baby,
And the universe slide from my side.

This is an image of liberation, and it is poetry that, like a child is born by caesarean section, cut out of the mother's body. Poetry has been gestating inside her:

I am sure it is unique, I am sure it is just what I want.
When I am quiet at my cooking I feel it looking, I feel it thinking.

It is typical of the method that Plath had developed in her poems from this period that different patterns of images should criss-cross through the poem, interacting upon one another. Many of those images recur in other poems – the domestic interiors, the metaphors of childbirth, the hospital images, religious imagery including the annunciation, the last supper, the beheading of John the Baptist, the piercing of Christ's side and the crucifixion and resurrection. Threaded into the poem is the terrible conflict between man and woman:

Is it impossible for you to let something go and have it go whole?
Must you kill what you can?

The poem is full of oblique references to other poems and to episodes in Plath's own life, her suicide attempt ('After all I am alive only by accident'), the animal quality she associates with Hughes and the death of her desire for him ('It must be a tusk there, a ghost column') or her dead father, who she associates with the dead king in *The Tempest* ('I would not mind if it was bones, or a pearl button').

The uniqueness of Plath's poetry makes it hard to define and equally hard to assess. In terms of successors, her poetry did not result in a school of Platheans, and her voice remains unique. Her antecedents likewise are difficult to pinpoint. She has been compared to Emily Dickinson, though in terms of her use of images she is closer to other American poets such as Walt Whitman and Ezra Pound. One writer who she resembles is the Argentinian poet who also died young, in 1972, Alejandra Pizarnik, and it is perhaps not too far-fetched to see the line of American poetry that runs from

Whitman through the imagists down to Plath running also in a parallel track through the work of many Latin American poets, given the huge impact of Whitman following his translation into Spanish. Like Whitman, Plath also created her own distinctive poetic universe.

3
God, Nature and Writing

There are notable differences between Sylvia Plath's earlier poetry and the poems written in the last 18 months of her life, differences not only of subject matter and imagery but also, especially, of form. This has led some critics to see her early poetry (the Juvenilia of the *Collected Poems* or the poems published in her lifetime in the volume *The Colossus*) as a prelude to her later work. Suzanne Juhasz, for example, notes how many commentators have analysed these poems in terms of their being influenced by other writers (mainly Theodore Roethke, Wallace Stevens, Dylan Thomas) and adds her own comment that 'this is a glittery, brilliant, self-conscious poetry of surface, a cold poetry'.[1]

Certainly the poems of *The Colossus* do show a concern for trying out different forms, for experimenting with imagery. They are often self-consciously intellectual poems, testing the reader's capacity to pick up on allusion and to join the writer in complex games that are played with words. But it is a pity to set these poems against the poems in the *Ariel* volume with a view to evaluating them less highly. A more constructive approach, it seems to me, is to consider those poems in which Sylvia Plath is consciously experimenting, as a stage in her development as a poet. Since writing was for her a craft, something that could be improved by hard work and concentrated effort, it is unfair to compare poems written at such different stages of her development of that craft. The organisation of the present book is an attempt to break away from that kind of evaluative reading of her poetry, by looking at some of the poems, together with prose work, under a set of general headings. I have chosen to use the *Collected Poems*, rather than to keep to the individual collections, and in this way I hope to show how certain lines are developed *through* her poetry, running from some of the earliest pieces to the later ones.

In a short piece entitled 'A Comparison', written for the BBC Home Service *The World of Books* programme in 1962, Sylvia Plath discusses the differences between writing novels and writing poetry. Painting a picture of the novelist as a woman who observes and details anything that she comes across in her daily life as potential novel material, she goes on to stress the time difference between the two types of writing. For the novelist, time is her business and she can choose the time she takes. For the poet, on the contrary, time is finite:

> How shall I describe it? – a door opens, a door shuts. In between you have had a glimpse: a garden, a person, a rainstorm, a dragon-fly, a heart, a city...

And there is really so little room! So little time! The poet becomes an expert packer of suitcases:

> *The apparition of these faces in the crowd;*
> *Petals on a wet black bough.*

There it is: the beginning and the end in one breath. How would the novelist manage that?[2]

The poem, Sylvia Plath tells us, can come in the instant of opening and closing a door. It is a moment of contact, of impact, 'a closed fist' to use her own image, compared to the 'open hand' of the novel. And while that open hand can bring in all kinds of details, the closed fist 'excludes and stuns'. The power of poetry, she argues, is not through its all-encompassing nature but through its spareness and the force of its point of impact. And the poet learning the craft of writing has to discover how to focus that power in the tiny interspace of time allowed.

Ted Hughes has left an account of Sylvia Plath's attempts to discover and shape that power. In his Notes on the Chronological Order of her poems[3] he suggests that her poems should ideally be read as an entity:

> I think it will be of service if I point out just how little of her poetry is 'occasional', and how faithfully her separate poems build up into one long poem.... The poems are chapters in a mythology... the world of her poetry is one of emblematic visionary events, mathematical symmetries, clairvoyance and metamorphoses. Her poetry escapes ordinary analysis in the way clairvoyance and mediumship do...

He also describes her method of writing, slowly and painstakingly, carefully shaping her poems until she came to a version that satisfied her:

> She wrote her first poems very slowly, Thesaurus open on her knee, in her large, strange handwriting, like a mosaic, where every letter stands separate within the work, a hieroglyph to itself. If she didn't like a poem, she scrapped it entire. She rescued nothing of it. Each poem grew complete from its own root, in that laborious inching way, as if she were working out a mathematical problem, chewing her lips, putting a thick dark ring of ink around each word that stirred for her on the page of the Thesaurus.

One of her earlier poems, 'Sonnet: To Time', is typical of the careful crafting of form and material that characterises so much of her work. It is divided into three four-line rhyming stanzas and a final couplet, seven pairs of rhymes in all. Each stanza marks a shift in perspective: so in the first stanza, the key pronoun is the collective *we*; in the second there is a shift to *I*; in the third there is an implicit *you*, subject of the imperative verbs – *cry/weep*; and in the last couplet there is a final shift to an impersonal third-person statement:

> Time is a great machine of iron bars
> That drains eternally the milk of stars.

Each stanza is structured around precise sets of images: the first stanza contains precious stones and jewelled clocks but also steel cars that bring death and artificial neon lights. The second stanza repeats the word 'steel', this time with reference to an entire city with plastic windows, but introduces the savagery of the natural world, 'the lone wind' that reminds the I-speaker of 'exclusion'. The third stanza refers to the lost world of myth, a pagan girl 'left picking olives / beside a sun blue sea', a thousand dead kings, a legendary dragon and commands that these lost images be mourned. Then, finally, in the couplet, comes the image of time as a machine, part of the contemporary world that destroys the magic of the imagination.

This is a poem about loss of beauty, about the corrupting influence of life in modern cities. But it is also a poem about loneliness and the choice of imagery refers outwards to sex-role conflicts too. The wind is male, it is 'his' voice that cries exclusion to the I-speaker,

and the first image of the mythic past that is introduced in the third
stanza is that of a woman who has been abandoned:

> So cry for the pagan girl left picking olives

And in the final couplet, time is portrayed as an iron machine that
drains away the life-giving milk of stars, female-produced source of
nourishment.

From this early poem, a vital feature of Sylvia Plath's writing
technique can be discerned. The poem shows a very clear sense of
structure, where rhyme, stanza, line length and imagery are all carefully patterned in making a consistent whole. Despite the speed
with which she apparently wrote many of her later poems these
earlier poems are, in the most literal sense of the word, crafted. She uses
the form of the poem to shape the experience she wants to convey;
not for her the notion that freedom of expression is somehow linked
to the idea of 'free' verse.

In an essay on Sylvia Plath's poetic technique, John F. Nims suggests
that 'without the drudgery of *The Colossus*, the triumph of *Ariel* is
unthinkable'.[4] He argues that nothing in these poems is accidental –
patterns of rhyme, rhythm, imagery and sound are all carefully
chosen and interrelated. Sometimes that conscious patterning seems
heavy-handed; in 'Firesong', written in 1956, for example, the use of
archaic language and staccato rhythms interferes with the material
contents:

> Sweet salts warped stem
> of weeds we tackle towards way's rank ending;
> scorched by red sun
> we heft globed flint, racked in veins' barbed bindings;

There are conscious echoes here of Gerard Manley Hopkins and the
Anglo-Saxon revival. The feeling of this poem is of a writer who is
consciously imitating other poets, trying out poetic devices on her
readers. The images, powerful though they are, take second place to
the patterns of repetition, alliteration, sound sequence and syllable
counts around which the poem is based. The overall impression
is of a slightly overdone painting, with just a little too much conscious
ornament.

But one thing is very clear from Sylvia Plath's experiments with
form – she conceives of poetry as word-craft, as a medium through

which experience can be shaped and represented. The vogue for supposedly spontaneous writing has passed her by and she dismisses what she perceives as false spontaneity:

> I *cannot* sympathize with these cries from the heart that are informed by nothing except, you know, a needle or a knife, or whatever it is. I believe one should be able to control and manipulate experiences, even the most terrifying, like madness, like being tortured.[5]

What lies behind Sylvia Plath's opinions is the profound question that so many writers face – what form should they choose through which to transmit experience. Sylvia Plath seems to have seen herself primarily as a prose writer and to have considered her poetry (at least in the early years of her writing) as a marginal activity. As a result, she struggled for years trying to write saleable stories, pushing the poetry back into another area of her writing experience. Gradually she came to write poetry with greater frequency and with increasing self-confidence, perhaps realising that the brevity of the poem, that moment of the door opening and shutting, did offer an opportunity to focus certain kinds of experience sharply and without any extraneous details. The early experiments with poetic devices show that she was concerned to try out the range of possibilities open to her within poetry. In a letter to her mother of 29 April 1956, she writes:

> I know that within a year I shall publish a book of 33 poems which will hit the critics violently in some way or another. My voice is taking shape, coming strong. Ted says he never read poems by a woman like mine; they are strong and full and rich – not quailing and whining like Teasdale or simple lyrics like Millais; they are working, sweating, heaving poems born out of the way words should be said . . .

In her study of the comparative influences between Ted Hughes and Sylvia Plath, Margaret Uroff suggests that up to the time of their meeting, Sylvia Plath had only two subjects, doomsday and love 'frequently intertwined and conveyed in painstakingly ornate language and forms'.[6] She sees Plath's nature poetry as heavily influenced by her husband but sees also that both poets helped one another to explore different avenues in their writing.

Nevertheless, from Plath's letters home, one interesting feature is the amount of emphasis she seems to have placed on Ted Hughes' poetry in comparison with her own. In a dramatic adaptation for television of the letters, a striking point of repetition is the praise of Hughes as a poet.[7] In the letter quoted above, Sylvia Plath quotes Ted Hughes' comment in terms of the originality of her poems for a woman. It is not too far-fetched to suggest that at least in the early years of her writing, Sylvia Plath felt an ambiguity in the fact of being both a woman and a poet, as if the writing of poetry were not strictly a woman's activity. Only later, in the 'blood jet' poems of the last two years of her life, do the entities of woman and of poet appear to fuse without any difficulty.

'Sonnet: To Time' also reveals another essential feature of Sylvia Plath's poetic technique – the intricate interweaving of a range of meanings, making it impossible to paraphrase the poem, to say 'what it is about'. Her poems are structured in a kaleidoscopic manner, with a central image or set of images and patterns of movement radiating out from that central core. Each poem opens up different sets of associations for the reader and those sets of associations shift with each subsequent reading. As an example, let us take a poem written in 1956 and described by Sylvia Plath as 'one good poem it moves and is athletic: a psychic landscape',[8] 'Winter Landscape, with Rooks':

Water in the millrace, through a sluice of stone,
plunges headlong into that black pond
where, absurd and out-of-season, a single swan
floats chaste as snow, taunting the clouded mind
which hungers to haul the white reflection down.

The austere sun descends above the fen,
an orange cyclops-eye, scorning to look
longer on this landscape of chagrin;
feathered dark in thought, I stalk like a rook,
brooding as the winter night comes on.

Last summer's reeds are all engraved in ice
as is your image in my eye; dry frost
glazes the window of my hurt; what solace
can be struck from rock to make heart's waste
grow green again? Who'd walk in this bleak place?

On one level, the poem offers a set of pictorial images: a single white swan, floating on a dark pond formed by the water of a millrace; a winter sun setting over the fens; ice in the reeds at the edge of the pond. This is the immediate landscape, one which anyone standing near the poet might see. But there are other pictorial images too, created not through description but through metaphor. The water, the swan, the sun, the iced-up reeds are all presented as direct statements of reality but the rook in verse 2 and the frost in verse 3 are not. Significantly, both these metaphoric images appear in conjunction with a personal pronoun – '*I* stalk like a rook'; 'dry frost/ glazes the window of *my* hurt'. The poet compares herself to a rook, brooding over the land as winter comes on, she has transposed herself into what she is describing, no longer describing what she sees. And having done this, all the phrases linked to the rook assume a set of connotations that take the reader beyond the pictorial and into a state of mind – phrases such as 'feathered dark, brooding, stalk' become much more than descriptive language. Another set of signs has entered the poems.

In the third verse, this process is continued. The reeds engraved in ice are directly compared to 'your image in my eye'. Frost glazing a window is introduced metaphorically to describe pain and the poem ends with two questions, both inviting negative answers. The winter will end and the spring will return but what solace can restore 'heart's waste'? And who indeed would walk in a place such as the one we have visited through the poem – the place inside the speaker's mind, rather than the place depicted in the first verse?

The first reading of the poem takes the reader through these various stages and leaves her sharing the poet's bleak landscape. But subsequent readings change that impression. Michael Riffaterre has discussed the ways in which all subsequent readings of a poem carry with them the signs of the initial reading and so inevitably alter those readings.[9] If we go back to this poem and look at it again, the first verse can no longer be read as descriptive. Instead, a series of metaphoric words leap off the page – *plunges, headlong, black, absurd, out of season, taunting, clouded, hungers, haul down* – and the second verse continues this process, introducing associations of death and horror in the 'cyclops-eye' of the sun. Now the poem begins to read more like an account of different mental states in which the speaker in the first verse is stirred by the beauty of the swan into black thoughts. The reference to chastity and the statement that the 'clouded mind' wants to destroy that 'white reflection' carries connotations of lost innocence or purity and a sense of bitterness at that loss. The I-speaker-rook in the second verse does not fly but stalks broodingly across 'this landscape of chagrin'. In the third verse, the use of the pronoun 'your' suggests that this might be a poem about unrequited or lost love, someone that the speaker of the poem has lost, together with the memories of summer and happiness.

The complexity of the layers of meaning and the way in which all the connotative systems interchange make it impossible to attribute a single theme to this poem. Clearly, it is a 'nature' poem in the simplest sense of the term but it is also a thought poem, an exploration of states of mind. Sylvia Plath writes poetry that can be compared to parable, since it takes place on several levels simultaneously.

In a short piece commissioned by the *London Magazine* in 1962 she tries to explain the sources of her poetic technique. Noting that she is preoccupied with the huge issues of nuclear warfare and the relationship between big business and militarism in America, she states nevertheless that she does not choose to write overtly about these issues. They influence her 'in a sidelong fashion' but

> My poems do not turn out to be about Hiroshima, but about a child forming itself finger by finger in the dark. They are not about the terrors of mass extinction, but about the bleakness of the moon over a yew tree in a neighbouring graveyard. Not about the testaments of tortured Algerians, but about the night thoughts of a tired surgeon.[10]

The yew tree stands out in her poetry as a powerful image and nowhere more so than in a poem dated 22 October 1961, 'The Moon and the Yew Tree'. This is a less consciously shaped poem in terms of rhyme schemes and immediately apparent structures but a very complex poem in terms of its patterning of images, a typical feature of her poems of this period. The central image is the tree:

> The yew tree points up. It has a Gothic shape.
> The eyes lift after it and find the moon.

But this description comes not at the start of the poem but at the beginning of the third verse. Before that, the landscape that is depicted is presented entirely in terms of metaphor. The first lines of the poem offer not the physical but the allegorical aspect of the yew tree and the moon:

> This is the light of the mind, cold and planetary.
> The trees of the mind are black. The light is blue.

The moon and the yew tree of the mind coexist with the moon and the yew tree that Sylvia Plath could see from her bedroom window in Devon. And the real and imagined objects set in motion a whole set of associations, presented through the poem as images. It would be too simple to say that the poem documents a chain reaction of associations; rather it is a poem in which thought processes are shaped and set down. The poem, in other words, tries to approximate the way in which thoughts move and memories intersect one another. The poet sets out to do this in four seven-line stanzas. The whole process is therefore one of implosion. Thoughts that move around freely in time and space are funnelled back into the 28 lines of the poem and are then released through the reader's response. It is not too far-fetched to see this kind of poetry as sacramental, in the way that the act of taking communion is also a moment of channelling enormity into a precisely determined form, which then assumes other meanings for the communicant.

The first verse sketches in the tree, the moon, the cemetery ('a row of headstones') within the mind and culminates in the line: 'I cannot see where there is to get to.' The second verse starts with this predicament and extends it:

> The moon is no door. It is a face in its own right,
> White as a knuckle and terribly upset.
> It drags the sea after it like a dark crime; it is quiet
> With the O-gape of complete despair. I live here.

There are two kinds of language operating in these lines (and throughout the whole poem) – the language of metaphor and the colloquial language of simple statement. The moon 'drags the sea after it like a dark crime' but it is also just 'terribly upset'. After the third line describing the anguish of the moon, comes the three-word statement 'I live here' that cannot be read without the connotations set up previously. Those three words, the shortest sentence in the poem, break the sequence of lines describing the moon and announce the next sequence of lines containing a set of images of religion and of the Holy Mother in particular. The church bells are also described in the two languages:

> Eight great tongues affirming the Resurrection,
> At the end, they soberly bong out their names.

The third verse begins with the yew tree again, this time with associations of Christianity in its Gothic shape. The moon now is another
persona:

> The moon is my mother. She is not sweet like Mary.
> Her blue garments unloose small bats and owls.
> How I would like to believe in tenderness...

There are two mothers here; the primitive mother of the night and
the virginal mother of Christianity and the poet seems to suggest
that it is the former that has a stronger claim over her, despite her
yearnings for belief in tenderness. The next six lines take up that
image of holiness and gentleness presented in terms not of life and
movement but of statuesque coldness and silence as the poet depicts
the effigies of saints inside the church. Those effigies are 'all blue'.
'Their hands and faces still with holiness'. There is no salvation here,
there is coldness and distance.

The fourth verse begins with the statement: 'I have fallen a long
way'. The verb 'fallen' carries with it associations of the fall from
grace, of a movement out of Christian salvation. In the third line of the
poem there is a direct reference to God: 'The grasses unload their
griefs on my feet as if I were God'. The God-poet in the fourth verse has
fallen from wherever she was before. There is no communication
between this fallen being and the vague, cold saints who float 'on
their delicate feet over the cold pews'. But any reading of the poem that
sees its theme as that of a lament for lost salvation would founder on
the last two lines if not before. After the images of the saints inside
their church, the poem returns to the moon and the tree:

> The moon sees nothing of this. She is bald and wild.
> And the message of the yew tree is blacknesss – blackness and silence.

The dichotomy in this poem is between two sets of mental images –
the images of the Christian faith, with its belief in resurrection and its
effigies of the mother of God, and the images of nature, personified
in the yew tree and the moon, male and female symbols in their
uprightness and circularity respectively that offer no prescription
for salvation, nothing but silence, blackness and themselves.

Where is the poet's own position vis-à-vis these two polarities?
The personal pronoun is present right through the poem but does
not intrude very forcefully. If we take out the five moments when

the *I* pronoun is used and string them together in a continuous narrative, what emerges is: 'The grasses unload their griefs on my feet as if I were God. I simply cannot see where there is to get to. I live here. How I would like to believe in tenderness. I have fallen a long way'. The thread through this narrative is not hard to follow. The poet declares her position by her non-alignment. Like the moon and the yew tree she exists, part of the universe in which they also move. And the placing of the *I* sentences through the poem causes them to be read as linked to the idea of suffering that is present in the depiction of the moon. There seems to be a fusion between the moon and the *I* of the poem, though this is never made explicit. The yew tree carries the message of blackness and silence; the moon oversees it all and cares for nothing except herself.

In 'A Comparison', Sylvia Plath talks about the way in which the image of the yew tree came to take over the poem in her view:

> I did, once, put a yew tree in. And that yew tree began, with astounding egotism, to manage and order the whole affair. It was not a yew tree by a church on a road past a house in a town where a certain woman lived…and so on, as it might have been, in a novel. Oh no. It stood squarely in the middle of my poem, manipulating its dark shades, the voices in the churchyard, the clouds, the birds, the tender melancholy with which I contemplated it – everything! I couldn't subdue it. And, in the end, my poem was a poem about a yew tree. That yew tree was just too proud to be a passing black mark in a novel.[11]

Recalling the poem in this way, Sylvia Plath adds another dimension to the reading. When I went back to the poem after first reading this, I found a whole new set of signs creeping into the reading. She describes it as primarily a poem about a yew tree, and a proud, manipulative yew tree at that. All kinds of associations of maleness now enter into the reading, associations that had previously been absent of value judgement. That the yew tree could be seen as a phallic symbol seemed obvious; that it was somehow trying to control and 'with astounding egotism' take over the poem had never occurred to me. Reading the poem in the light of this new set of associations, the wildness of the moon and the suffering of the moon also became more explicitly feminised, as also did the refusal of the moon to participate. The moon of this poem drags the sea 'after it' but is nevertheless 'a face in its own right'. By the last lines of the poem, the moon is no longer 'It' but 'she', bald and lunatic, tracking her pathway across the sky. These associations add another dimension to Ted Hughes' comment that this poem, written at his suggestion, had depressed him greatly.

In her book *Chapters in a Mythology: The Poetry of Sylvia Plath*, Judith Kroll talks about the moon as a central symbol in Plath's poetry. She points out that there are more than a hundred direct references to the moon in the poems and argues that the moon functions

> as her emblematic muse – her Moon-muse – which symbolizes the deepest source and inspiration of the poetic vision, the poet's vocation, her female biology, and her role and fate as protagonist in a tragic drama; and, through the use of a lunar iconography, it gives concrete form to the particular spirit of the mythicized biography.[12]

Kroll discusses the enormous impact that reading Robert Graves' *The White Goddess* had on Sylvia Plath's poetry. It was Ted Hughes who introduced her to the book, which had become the subject of a cult following. Graves' book appealed both because of its celebration of poetry and of the idea of the poet but also because of his investigations into the mythical sources of the creation of poetry. The White Goddess – the source of all poetry and of all life, the sublime muse – stands in direct contrast to the male, fatherly God of Christianity and rationalism. She is not constant and fixed but fluid and in perpetual movement, symbolised by the phases of the moon. The moon goddess is, simultaneously, goddess of three stages of female existence – she is the virgin huntress of the new moon, the pregnant mother of the full moon and the wild hag of the waning moon. Her colours are white, red and black – whiteness being associated with purity but also with barrenness; red being associated with blood; both life blood and menstrual blood; and black being associated with decay, death and mourning. Her element is the sea, she controls the tides and all liquids. She rules the Underworld and concerns of birth, procreation and death; she rules the Earth and concerns of the changing seasons; she rules the Sky and concerns of the changing moon. The totality of the moon-goddess' power meant that the power of a male god was negligible. She had a lover but his power diminished every year as the power of the sun faded in late autumn, whilst her power remained constant. Only gradually did the patriarchal system come to take precedence and the White Goddess was dethroned and set up as an antagonist to the patriarchal system.

It is easy to see why this mythology should hold such appeal. The symbols of the White Goddess can be used in multiple ways and the simultaneous existence of the goddess as virgin, mother and hag offers enormous possibilities for poetry. Sylvia Plath has incorporated the triple patterning of the White Goddess into her own writing, seeing in its intricacies a solution to the perennial problem felt by women, that of fragmentation. The disparity that she felt between her ambition to write, her desire to be fulfilled as a woman through a successful relationship with a man and her need for a child, all of which seemed to be in conflict with each other, could be resolved through the idea of simultaneity that avoids resolution. In *The Bell Jar* she describes the horrors of fragmentation in a nightmare image:

I saw my life branching out before me like the green fig-tree in the story.

From the tip of every branch, like a fat purple fig, a wonderful future beckoned and winked. One fig was a husband and a happy home and children, and another fig was a famous poet and another fig was a brilliant professor, and another fig was E Gee, the amazing editor, and another fig was Europe and Africa and South America, and another fig was Constantin and Socrates and Attila and a pack of other lovers with queer names and off-beat professions, and another fig was an Olympic lady crew champion, and beyond and above these figs were many more figs I couldn't quite make out. I saw myself sitting in the crotch of this fig-tree, starving to death, just because I couldn't make up my mind which of the figs I would choose. I wanted each and every one of them, but choosing one meant losing all the rest, and, as I sat there, unable to decide, the figs began to wrinkle and go black, and, one by one, they plopped to the ground at my feet.[13]

On another level, the image of the fig tree offers the reader an insight into Sylvia Plath's obsessive desire to succeed in everything. Fragmented though life may be, Esther Greenwood (protagonist of the novel), like Sylvia Plath, wants the best fig on every bough.

The myth of the Triple Goddess does at least offer a ray of hope to women like Esther Greenwood, who find themselves forced to fragment their existence in such a way, because the Goddess is *simultaneously* a virgin, mother and hag and the three entities are in harmony and not in opposition to one another as they are in Esther's nightmare. Judith Kroll makes large claims for the impact of the White Goddess myth on Sylvia Plath's poetry but what is undeniable is the recurrence of images of the goddess, with her tripartite persona and her three symbolic colours throughout the poems.

Although the White Goddess myth offers a way out of fragmentation, into a notion of femaleness as multiple, it also raises the problem of relationship with the male principle. As the Goddess' power wanes, so Graves traces the growth of patriarchy and the worship of things male. Maleness is therefore the enemy, it is the force that destroys the Goddess, forcing her cult underground. And throughout the poetry, there is a recurrence of a sinister, dominant male figure – the colossus, the Zoo Keeper, the Jailer, the Nazi, the vampire, the bridegroom, the father:

> And your neat mustache
> And your Aryan eye, bright blue.
> Panzer-man, panzer-man, O You –
>
> Not God but a swastika
> So black no sky could squeak through.
> Every woman adores a Fascist,
> The boot in the face, the brute
> Brute heart of a brute like you.
>
> 'Daddy', 12 October 1962

> Your voice my ear-ring,
> Flapping and sucking, blood-loving bat.
> That is that. That is that.
> You peer from the door,
> Sad hag. 'Every woman's a whore.
> I can't communicate.'
>
> 'Lesbos', 18 October 1962

> Herr God, Herr Lucifer
> Beware
> Beware.
>
> Out of the ash
> I rise with my red hair
> And I eat men like air.
>
> 'Lady Lazarus', 23–29 October 1962

The moon and the yew tree of the poem are therefore not partners but antagonists, symbols of the struggle between female and male that pervades Sylvia Plath's work. Long before the break-up of her marriage and the poems written explicitly around this crisis in her life, the battle-lines are drawn up. In an early poem entitled 'Bluebeard', the key lines repeated three times are: 'I am sending back the key/ that let me into bluebeard's study'. Sexual relations are interpreted in terms of struggle; and with the White Goddess myth, the domestic and the cosmic conflicts combine.

Robert Graves' book raises a second problem for the woman poet. He finds the two roles incompatible and struggles to explain what he means by this:

> woman is not a poet: she is either a Muse or she is nothing. This is not to say that a woman should refrain from writing poems; only, that she should write as a woman not as if she were an honorary man. The poet was originally the *mystes*, or ecstatic devotee of the Muse; the women who took part in her rites were her representatives... poetry in its archaic setting in fact, was either the moral and religious law laid down for man by the nine-fold Muse, or the ecstatic utterance of the man in furtherance of this law and in glorification of the Muse. It is the imitation of male poetry that causes the false ring in the work of almost all women poets.

So how then, is a woman to write poetry? Graves offers her two choices – either be 'a silent Muse' and inspire male poets to write or 'be the Muse in a complete sense':

> she should be in turn Arianrhod, Blodeuwedd and the Old Sow of Maenawr Penardd who eats her farrow, and should write in each of these capacities with antique authority. She should be the visible moon: impartial, loving, severe, wise.[14]

Dying as she did in 1963, Sylvia Plath never knew that so soon afterwards the problem of what and how women write was to become such a crucial matter and was to be debated by so many other women. Suzanne Juhasz, Adrienne Rich, Tillie Olsen to name but three writers who are also critics have all described the problem of the double bind for women – that the forms and language of poetry are determined and defined by a male tradition and that the criteria for assessing both the subject matter and the shape of writing are also laid down by men. Outside this system, women are marginalised and can only try to break into this world. In the annals of literary history, women poets are described as a minority, frequently also as minor. Only a few women poets are allowed a place in the pantheon of great (male) poets and then they are often decried for their overly 'feminine' way of writing.

Other women have gone even further. The French and Italian group of post-feminist writers – Luce Irigaray, Hélène Cixous, Julia Kristeva, Xavière Gauthier, Elisabetta Rasy, Marina Mizzau – have all argued that language itself mirrors the male-dominated structuring of the world. The Logos – reason, learning, the Word – has come to be equated with the Phallus, symbol of maleness. Women are therefore completely trapped for the very ideas they have about language and literary forms have been determined for them and belong to others. As Mary Jacobus says, summarising the dilemma:

> Can women adopt traditionally male-dominated modes of writing and analysis to the articulation of female oppression and desire? Or should we rather reject tools that may simply re-inscribe our marginality and deny the specificity of our experience, instead forging others of our own? – reverting perhaps to the traditionally feminine in order to revalidate its forms (formlessness?) and pre-occupations – rediscovering subjectivity; the language of feeling; ourselves.[15]

The discussions on the nature of women's writing, begun again with the revival of feminism in the late sixties, have gone further than ever before in trying to redefine the problems and work out strategies for resolving them. Sylvia Plath was never able to know that; for her, there remained her own intuition, the discovery of her own voice and the inadequately expressed version of the woman-poet problem as set out by Graves. What he seems to be struggling to say is something very similar to what later feminist writers were to say also: that in order to write both as woman and as poet, it is necessary to find a centre, to find a voice that will carry the dual role of poet and muse, a duality that is totally outside the experience of any male poet and therefore totally beyond his powers of expression.

Suzanne Juhasz suggests that Sylvia Plath began to do this in her last poems and explains her reasons for believing this:

For Plath, poetry had always been symbolic of action. In *The Colossus*, she had used language to impose an order upon experience, but the order in her poems contradicted her vision of reality as fragmented and perpetually disintegrating. Only in a poem could the world be composed and controlled, and so poetry was artificial: it lied. In the later poetry, she begins to tell the truth. When she comes to see that reality resides in her own mind, words and poems become as real as anything else. The expression of her vision in words unleashes reality, for her poems describe what is real: her own consciousness. The action that is poetry is recognised as symbolic action (she never ceases to know the *difference* between art and life), but the symbols now reflect rather than counteract her own life.[16]

Juhasz quotes Sylvia Plath in an interview, talking about her earlier poems and saying that they now 'quite bore me'. One of the reasons she gives for this feeling of boredom is her discovery that she cannot read any of the poems from *The Colossus* aloud any more. 'I didn't write them to be read aloud', she explains and contrasts them with her most recent writing of poems that have got to be said. The patterns of sound and rhythm that she carefully crafted into the earlier poems now emerge without that conscious working. Ann Sexton uses a metaphor of release from imprisonment to describe the process of change between the first poems and the last:

> Those early poems were all in a cage (and not even her own cage at that). I felt she hadn't found a voice of her own, wasn't in truth, free to be herself...at the end, Sylvia burst from her cage and came riding straight out.[17]

The early poems are poems of exploration. Sylvia Plath experiments with fixed forms, testing their potential for flexibility, working within accepted canons of poetry. She also experiments with material for poetry, discovering the myth of the all-powerful female goddess and her fall from power and developing many of the themes and images that were to recur throughout her writing. What comes across most sharply is the conscious *searching* in these poems, both linguistically, as she stretches and moulds language into startling shapes and forms, and in the choice of subject matter. Behind many of the poems are specific visual pictures – the view from a window or across a moorland, Old Ella Mason and her eleven cats, the local farmer's prize sow, a snowman, moments in her everyday life that struck her enough for them to serve as the basis of a poem.

There are also the poems written about pictures – 'Conversation among the Ruins' and 'The Disquieting Muses' based on paintings by Giorgio de Chirico, 'Virgin in a Tree', 'Perseus', 'Battle-scene', 'The Ghost's Leavetaking' based on paintings by Paul Klee, 'Yadwigha, on a Red Couch, Among Lilies' based on Douanier Rousseau's painting, *The Dream*. In all these poems, the process is similar to the implosive technique of 'The Moon and the Yew Tree', where the object of the poet's gaze triggers off sequence after sequence of images, whose great range is carefully channelled and controlled within the frame of the poem. There is the feeling of a writer with a lot to say, looking for subjects that will trigger off chains of perception. The metaphor I use in defining these early poems for myself is that they remind me of someone learning to dance. When a woman who is an intellectual in the sense of having been part of the educational system and desiring to shape that system for future students starts to write poetry, it is unavoidable that there should be some deliberate use of all that academic training. Likewise, if that woman were to learn to dance, she would begin by intellectualising movement, by thinking it all through consciously. The result of this kind of learning is that the woman *does* learn to dance, she learns the steps and can move herself around in space in time to the music. But there is a tiny hiatus between the thought and the step. When she has finally mastered the art of dancing, that pause will no longer happen; the body will move without the conscious mind telling it how to go. Movement and thought will have become one.

This, it seems to me, is what happens to the poet who has fully absorbed the craft of word-making. There comes a point when there is no need to seek conscious subjects for poems nor to try out different forms, for form and subject emerge simultaneously in a complete unified whole. Those early poems by Sylvia Plath 'about' specific things, whether landscapes, animals, paintings or people, are often beautifully crafted works and the fact that so many were published as she sent them out to Journals shows the positive response they aroused in many readers. They have suffered from negative evaluation because they have so often been placed in comparison with the final poems she wrote, when they do, indeed, appear more restricted, more caged. But then the early poems and the last poems had a very different function for their creator. When she first started to write poetry, she saw the poet as something outside herself, something that she might aspire to. Her letters show her strong feelings of enthusiasm for Ted Hughes' poetry, her delight and pride in his success as a poet. She talks about him as her teacher, describes how she typed his manuscripts for him, shared his irritation at rejections by editors. In a letter to her mother of 24 February 1957, describing the news they had received about 'The Hawk in the Rain' winning a major award, she writes:

> You know, it is, to the day, the anniversary of that fatal party where I met Ted! And I'd read his poems before and had a vision of how much I could do for him and with him. Genius will out...
>
> I am more happy than if it was my book published! I have worked so closely on these poems of Ted's and typed them so many countless times through revision after revision that I feel ecstatic about it all.
>
> I am so happy *his* book is accepted *first*. It will make it so much easier for me when mine is accepted – if not by the Yale Series, then by some other place. I can rejoice then, much more, knowing Ted is ahead of me. There is no question of rivalry, but only mutual joy and a sense of us doubling our prize-winning and creative output.

The feeling expressed in this letter obviously bothered Aurelia Plath, who unusually adds a footnote, in which she tells anecdotes about her daughter's belief in male superiority: 'From the time Sylvia was a very little girl, she catered to the male of any age so as to bolster his sense of superiority'. This footnote is curious and seems to express both a sense of irritation and a need for apology. Sylvia Plath's obvious delight in her husband's success, expressed in such voluble terms, seems to disturb her mother who, in the footnote, does not so much excuse as condemn her daughter for this attitude. Nevertheless, the attitude is consistent with Sylvia Plath's perceptions of herself and Ted Hughes as poets, as expressed in all her writings. She did not rate herself as a lesser writer than her husband, she simply saw him as a *poet*, herself as a writer who also wrote poetry.

The function of her own poetry at this time was therefore quite different from the function of poetry in the last months of her life. When she met Ted Hughes, she was still aiming to become an academic and a novelist and poetry was a way of learning more about the craft of writing and, probably, of sharing more with him. She tells her mother that he was persuading her to memorise a poem a day (letter of 9 January 1957) and the letters through the first part of 1957 are full of accounts of the progress her novel was making. Only in August of that year did she start writing poetry again, another carefully crafted piece that shows close thinking about content material and structure:

> I am at last writing my first poem for about six months, a more ambitious topic: a short verse dialogue which is supposed to sound just like conversation but is written in strict 7-line stanzas, rhyming ababcbc. It frees me from my writer's cramp and is at last a good subject – a dialogue over an Ouija board, which is both dramatic and philosophical. (6 August 1957)

Later, when the ordered pattern of her working life fell apart, the function of poetry was very different. She wrote out of a driving need to shape her fluctuating states of mind into poetry. In the days when she could control and discipline her working time, poetry had its place along with all the other parts of her life, but when first the pressures of small babies, then the collapse of her marriage and the need to earn a living alone eliminated that order and imposed other controls on her, writing poetry became something vastly different. That difference can be illustrated by two moments, from two poems, the one written in 1956, the other just a few days before she died. In the first poem, 'Conversation Among the Ruins' the last line asks the question 'What ceremony of words can patch the havoc?'. Chaos and despair are carefully controlled and the speaker does not lose grip on dignity. But in 'Words', that measured quality has gone and instead the four short verses strike with clenched fists. The final verse hits hardest of all:

> Words dry and riderless,
> The indefatigable hoof-taps.
> While
> From the bottom of the pool, fixed stars
> Govern a life.

The bareness of this poem heightens its impact. There is no sense at all of conscious crafting, of searching for effect. Instead there is a sense of spontaneity, of a poet using all the power she has stored up unconsciously, a sense of release.

The differences between the early poems and the later poems do not negate the continuity in all Sylvia Plath's writing. Reading her works today, we read them as part of the text that also comprises her letters, Journals and biography but even if we did not have access to all this additional material there would still be clear lines through the poetry, in terms of imagery, theme, patterning and language. At times certain images come to a prominence that is unique, elsewhere as in the case of roses, bees, the moon, for example, they recur constantly. One set of images that do change slightly, however, are the images relating to men and masculinity. The savage male figures of the later poems are prefigured in the early poems by images of weightiness, stoniness, stasis. These images add up to a collective image of males as figures of power that block and obstruct. There is the great head of Perseus, the old man of the sea with his conch shell 'deep among knuckles, shinbones/skulls' ('Full Fathom Five'), the hermit at Outermost House with his 'backbone unbendable' and, of course, the colossus.

The image of the colossus is a powerful one, combining as it does the two figures of husband and father. She had used the image in a 1956 poem, 'Letter to a Purist' – 'The grandiose colossus' who

> Stood astride
> The envious assaults of sea
>
> . . . .
> Has nothing on you,
> O my love...

It is a strong image, with its Shakespearean connotations (it was Mark Antony who was said to bestride the world like a colossus). In Sylvia Plath's handling of the image, it becomes a symbol of hugeness, across which the I-speaker of the poem crawls 'like an ant'. But it is a statue full of defects, incompletely constructed. The opening lines of the poem introduce this image:

> I shall never get you put together entirely,
> Pieced, glued, and properly jointed.

The colossus is the product of the I-speaker's creation, it is her task to maintain it, her life's work to keep it cleaned and repaired:

> Thirty years now I have labored
> To dredge the silt from your throat.

The pictorial images are striking, echoing Hieronymus Bosch, Max Ernst, Salvador Dali, all painters of nightmare visions where human-ised landscapes are fragmented and in dissolution. The first three stanzas contain images specifically of the great statue's decay. In the first stanza, the speaker protests her inability to complete the repair and complains about the barnyard noise of 'mule-bray, pig-grunt and bawdy cackles' that come from the mouth of the statue. It cannot utter any coherent, meaningful sound, and the second verse takes up this failed communication, contrasting what the colossus might think it is capable of – 'Perhaps you consider yourself an oracle' with the simple 'I am none the wiser'. The third verse contrasts the size of the colossus with the minuteness of the I-speaker, crawling across its brow, and develops Images of death – 'weedy acres, skull-plates, white tumuli'.

In the fourth stanza the poem shifts gear. Three new motifs are introduced: the doomed House of Atreus of the Oresteia, the military might of ancient Rome and the link between the statue and the father:

> A blue sky out of the Oresteia
> Arches above us. O father, all by yourself
> You are pithy and historical as the Roman Forum.

The last two stanzas move around in time, into the past and into the future. The process of construction of the colossus is hinted at:

> It would take more than a lightning-stroke
> To create such a ruin.

The speaker shelters in the left ear of the monument, watching the sun rise 'under the pillar of your tongue'. And in the last three lines, with the quiet assertions of present state of being, there is a suggestion of something being ended, of a future that will not involve waiting in vain for someone to come:

> My hours are married to shadow.
> No longer do I listen for the scrape of a keel
> On the blank stones of a landing.

Again, this is a psychic landscape poem. Some critics have read it as a poem in which Sylvia Plath explores her feelings about the memory of her long-dead father, a memory from which there can be no escape. Suzanne Juhasz, for example, reads the poem as a despairing statement about the poet's inability to free herself from her memories about her existence in a state of living death, in shadow. This is certainly a possible reading, but only if the poem is looked at in isolation from the rest of her work. If taken out of context, then it does indeed read as a poem about a dead father, looming hugely in the life of the scurrying little figure doomed to perpetually try to repair his effigy. The last three lines, in this reading, are slightly curious but could be taken to signify loss of hope, impossibility of escape.

But there is an alternative reading and it is one which can be made by looking at the poem as part of the single poem that Ted Hughes suggests is what her opus really is. In a letter to her mother, written on 29 November 1957, Sylvia Plath drew together the two men in her life:

> It is heaven to have someone like Ted who is so kind and honest and brilliant – always stimulating me to study, think, draw, and write. He is better than any teacher, even fills somehow that huge, sad hole I felt in having no father. I feel every day how wonderful he is and love him more and more.

And the last three lines of the poem can be read to suggest that the speaker is not condemned to eternal waiting, for someone else has already arrived in her life. The use of the verb 'married' in the third line of that last stanza seems particularly significant. The speaker's 'hours are married to shadow', the poem is married to another (male) poet who is teaching her to expand her own creativity, woman in her role as goddess is married to man, the dark Other with whom she is perpetually in conflict, the poem of time present waits in the shadow of its future reader. Not one of these possibilities is clearly marked as determinant, all are equally as possible and as far-fetched as a reader chooses them to be. Two things, though, remain clear from this poem – the great, ponderous weightiness of the male colossus, the figure that, whether father or husband or image from classical times, dwarfs the woman who tends it, and the imperfections of that crumbling effigy. The daughter/wife/acolyte/priestess scales across its forehead 'with gluepots and pails of Lysol', like an energetic housewife pausing for lunch in the litter and confusion of 'fluted bones and acanthine hair'. There is irony here and wit, rather than anguish. The woman tending the colossus knows her place, her duty and her history but is a long, long way from being crushed by it.

4

Writing the Family

Sylvia Plath was both daughter and mother, a dual role that recurs throughout her writing. Psychoanalytical critics have tried to show that her entire output is concerned with exorcising the figures of her dead father and possessive mother. Others, such as Alvarez, have suggested that her role of artist was somehow incompatible with her role as mother. Describing a meeting with her in 1960, he describes her as 'a lovely young housewife'. Later, meeting her again after the birth of Nicholas in 1962, he suggests that her 'new confident air' that made her no longer 'a housewifely appendage to a powerful husband' might have been linked to the fact that she had given birth to a son.[1] Both these positions seem to me to be both false and extreme. There are certainly attempts through the writing to rethink the poet's relationship with both her father and her mother and there are many poems and a good deal of prose that tackles the question of motherhood in its own right, but no evidence of psychosis in either. Had Sylvia Plath lived and been able to participate in the discussions on women and the family that were to follow ten years after her death, she would have found herself in the company of many other women, all wrestling with the same problems. The need to think through the roles of a woman as daughter to a man, as daughter to a woman, as mother in turn to a female and a male child is a central preoccupation of the literature produced by the women's movement of the late sixties and early seventies. Sylvia Plath was exceptional not because she was somehow deranged but because she was trying to confront those problems ahead of their time.

Linked to her writing about the family is her writing about writing. Again and again she uses the metaphor of pregnancy to talk about producing a poem or a story. In her Journal, an entry dated 7 July 1958 refers to 'the ghost of the unborn novel' as 'a Medusa-head' and throughout her writing the link is made between barrenness, sterility and inability to write. Her poem 'Stillborn', written in 1960, provides one of the clearest examples of her use of this metaphor.

The first line states the obvious: 'These poems do not live: It's a sad diagnosis' and goes on to describe those poems in terms of developing babies – 'They grew their toes and fingers well enough,/ their little foreheads bulged with concentration'. But the poem-foetuses, though 'proper in shape and number and every part', have no life; they lack the vital ingredient. Pickled in jars (the image of pickled foetuses is one which recurs through Sylvia Plath's writing, particularly prominent in *The Bell Jar*) they 'smile and smile and smile' in the second verse, a perception which changes to 'they stupidly stare and do not speak of her [their mother]' in the last line of the poem.

The image of the dead poem-foetuses is constant throughout, with each of the three stanzas supplying additional visual imagery. What changes is the point of view of the third-person narrative, which in the second stanza becomes a first-person narrative with the cry 'O I cannot understand what happened to them!'. The first stanza gives a description of the initial growth and development of the dead poems and offers the mother a way out:

> If they missed out on walking about like people
> It wasn't for any lack of mother-love.

The mother is not responsible for their death, she has not failed in her duty as a mother. But the second stanza introduces the I-speaker looking at the jars of pickling fluid whose contents smile back at her and the fourfold repetition of the word 'smile' stresses the incongruity of the act of smiling, and its associations of joyfulness, with the horror of what she sees. The language of the poem mirrors the description in *The Bell Jar*, Chapter 6, when Esther Greenwood is shown the cadaver room by her medical student boyfriend, Buddy Willard:

> After that, Buddy took me out into a hall where they had some big glass bottles full of babies that had died before they were born. The baby in the first bottle had a large white head bent over a tiny curled-up body the size of a frog. The baby in the next bottle was bigger and the baby next to that was bigger still and the baby in the last bottle was the size of a normal baby and he seemed to be looking at me and smiling a little piggy smile.[2]

It is that description which lies behind the first two lines of the third stanza which returns to the third-person narrative and develops the notion of the shapelessness and formlessness of the dead poems:

> They are not pigs, they are not even fish,
> Though they have a piggy and a fishy air –

Because they have not come to life, they have no recognisable form. They had begun to live in the womb and then stopped developing. Pickled in jars, their grotesque smiling can also be perceived as a stupid, silent stare, a glare of reproach at the mother who is 'near dead with distraction'. Only by the end of the poem does that mother-grief come out, expressed through the pain of silence and non-communication.

The link between sterility and blocked writing that is so strongly made in much of Sylvia Plath's writing takes on additional implications in the poems of the last months of her life. 'Thalidomide', a poem dated 8 November 1962, works on the horrific images of deformity that had recently come to light in the discovery that the drug, thalidomide, was causing physical malformations in unborn children. Written in the period when she was living apart from her husband (a letter dated 7 November to her mother describes how she had finally found a flat in London, in Yeats' former house, for herself and the children), the images of deformity can be read on several levels. Firstly, they relate to the immediate newspaper images, fresh in the minds of the British public at that time, and the I-speaker of the poem asks the question that millions of women must also have asked themselves:

> What glove
> What leatheriness
> Has protected
> Me from that shadow –

This is the poet in touch with the darkest fears of all pregnant women, that their child may somehow be growing deformed and crippled within the womb. But, in view of the recurrence of the foetus-poem-in-the-making metaphor that Sylvia Plath uses so frequently, this also becomes central to the development of the poem:

> All night I carpenter
> A space for the thing I am given,
> A love
> Of two wet eyes and a screech.

Making a poem, despite the care and the labour, the carpentering, can sometimes result in a monstrous birth. And the metaphor takes on a further dimension yet, if it is read in terms of the destruction of an ideal, planned-for love:

> White spit
> Of indifference!
> The dark fruits revolve and fall.

The poem ends with a whole range of densely packed metaphoric words:

> The glass cracks across,
> The image
> Flees and aborts like dropped mercury.

The mirror of perfection (and there may be an unconscious echo here of the Lady of Shallott, whose mirror 'cracked from side to side' when she broke the rules of her enchantment and reached out to a man whose indifference to her was to be her death) is broken, the ghastly choice facing the prospective mother is either to flee from her deformed offspring or abort it, to abandon the crippled ideal of love or attempt to flush it away. It is a powerful, moving blending of images that works in all kinds of ways.

The image of barrenness and idealism is developed further in a poem dated 28 January 1963, 'The Munich Mannequins'. The opening line of this poem is one of the best remembered of all Sylvia Plath's lines:

> Perfection is terrible, it cannot have children.

Starting here, the poem goes on to develop through a chain of images of desolation, coldness, loneliness and silence. Whiteness and sterility are the counter signs to redness and productivity, the 'blood jet' of poetry ('Kindness', written four days later) and the menstrual flow, described in line 6 as 'the flood of love'. The mannequins symbolise perfect women in that they represent the visual ideal image of what society declares to be beautiful but in the surreal straightness – 'orange lollies on silver sticks' – they are the antithesis of productive, pregnant roundness. The spilt menstrual blood in the opening lines of the poem is symbolic of waste and unfulfilled femininity:

Perfection is terrible, it cannot have children.
Cold as snow breath, it tamps the womb

Where the yew trees blow like hydras,
The tree of life and the tree of life

Unloosing their moons, month after month, to no purpose.
The bloodflood is the flood of love,

The absolute sacrifice.

Menstruation as waste is an image that Sylvia Plath refers to several times in her writing, most frequently in the period when she was hoping to become pregnant, having decided finally that she did want to have children. In her Journal entry for 20 March 1959, she notes:

Yesterday a nadir of sorts. Woke up to cat's early mewling around six. Cramps. Pregnant I thought. Not, such luck. After a long 40 day period of hope, the old blood cramps and spilt fertility. I had lulled myself into a fattening calm and this was a blow...

This Journal entry, recording as it does a particularly painful moment, one that is familiar to many women, shows how far Sylvia Plath linked the imagery of the blood flow to her own creativity/productivity and it shows also that this is an image that is fundamentally ambiguous. The bloodflow and the creative flow are sometimes synonymous but elsewhere that flow of blood is a reminder of non-productivity, in the sense that it is a sign that conception has not taken place. Reading the last poems, it seems to me that there is a suggestion that, despite the existence of her children, poetry has *become* her menstruation, for her actual monthly period must have been a regular reminder of how, without a man, she could not produce more children. Her Journal and her letters, especially during the early phase of her marriage, recount her desire for several children, for a future in which she and Ted Hughes would become both great writers and great parents, with many children. On 1 December 1962, she had written 'Childless Woman', a poem in which there seems to be a direct link between menstrual blood, unused in the making of new children, and words, used in the making of poems:

Spiderlike, I spin mirrors,
Loyal to my image,

Uttering nothing but blood –
Taste it, dark red!
And my forest

My funeral,
And this hill and this
Gleaming with the mouths of corpses.

It would be far too simplistic to suggest that childbearing and writing are antithetical to each other in Sylvia Plath's later work. That she tried so hard to balance these different parts of her life shows how concerned she was to have both and how her ideal state of existence would have been the achieving of that state of perfect equilibrium. The problem seems to have been that those two parts were so rarely balanced: for years, during the period of her studying and the start of her academic career, children represented a whole other state of being, one that she both aspired to and feared alternately. Then, with the birth of her daughter Frieda, came a brief phase of baby-centredness, when she stopped writing to concentrate on her mothering. In the late summer of 1960 her letters show a revival of concern for her work and some poems were written during these months, but then came the winter, her miscarriage, her appendicitis and, finally, the collapse of the marriage. The possibility of balance was over. *Crossing the Water*, dated 4 April 1962, is already full of images of ending. The final line 'This is the silence of astounded souls' prefigures the poems about the death of love that were to follow. It is a bitter irony that just as she began to realise her desire for several children and poetry, the relationship that was to have been the source of her ideal family disintegrated. The great last rush of poems are evidence of the failure of her attempts to balance the parts of her life that she needed for completeness.

The integration of her different roles as producer of texts and producer of children was something closely tied into her marriage. Before that, as the letters, Journal and novel testify, she tended to see childbearing and career as conflicting aims. In Chapter 18 of *The Bell Jar*, as Esther begins to recover from her breakdown, she thinks about her ambiguous feelings towards babies in general:

I leafed nervously through an issue of *Baby Talk*. The fat, bright faces of babies beamed up at me, page after page – bald babies, chocolate-coloured babies, Eisenhower-faced babies, babies rolling over for the first time, babies reaching for rattles, babies eating their first spoonful of solid food, babies doing all the tricky things it takes to grow up, step by step, into an anxious and unsettling world.

I smelt a mingling of Pabulum and sour milk and salt-cod-stinky diapers and felt sorrowful and tender. How easy having babies seemed to the women around me! Why was I so unmaternal and apart? Why couldn't I dream of devoting myself to baby after fat puling baby like Dodo Conway?

If I had to wait on a baby all day, I would go mad.[3]

The desire to have children seems to have been linked to Sylvia Plath's feelings for Ted Hughes, who represented the ideal man. Before meeting him, in her Journal, she had written about her feelings of resentment against men, who seemed able in her view to have the best of all worlds:

I am jealous of men – a dangerous and subtle envy which can corrode, I imagine, any relationship. It is an envy born of the desire to be active and doing, not passive and listening. I envy the man his physical freedom to lead a double life – his career, and his sexual and family life. I can pretend to forget my envy; no matter, it is there, insidious, malignant, latent.[4]

At that stage in her life, as a student at Smith College in 1951, it seemed impossible that there might be the same possibility of totality open to a woman. Throughout the early letters home, she seems to almost overemphasise the importance of her career side, of the stories and poems accepted for publication, the prizes she won. It has been suggested that she did this in her letters to her mother because that was principally what her mother wanted to hear; that may be so but nevertheless it also seems to have been something that she wanted to say. She was, after all, a product of the American middle-class dream of the post-war period, which saw education as the panacea of all ills, whether social or personal, and although she was able to grow beyond that perspective, it did exert a great influence over her in her formative years.

Carole Ferrier, the Australian feminist writer, describes the existential problems that Sylvia Plath faced very clearly.

Plath was in many ways a victim of the fifties and its ideology of the family. Women struggling to lead independent lives or pursue the ideal of being writers were under pressure to submerge themselves within monogamous marriage and create households straight out of the *Ladies' Home Journal*. Plath died just as the new wave of feminist theory began to surface with the rise of the women's movement and the publication of Betty Friedan's attempt to define 'the problem that has no name' in *The Feminine Mystique*. Plath, in common with women grappling then with the problems of developing feminist theory, was fighting her way in those poems of the early sixties towards a definition of what life within the middle-class nuclear family does to its members. Her distinctive mediation of the ideology of the family and of love in the fifties and early sixties can tell us a great deal about patriarchal attitudes and how women in general, and women writers in particular, can find ways to resist and triumph over them.[5]

One of the very early poems, 'Family Reunion', gives a portrait of a woman distanced from the aunts and uncles who gather together ('hear the clash of people meeting') and who can only participate in the charade of family unity by falsifying herself: 'I cast off my identity/and make the fatal plunge'. Several years later in 'Candles' (17 October 1960), a poem written after she had given birth to Frieda in April, Sylvia Plath again explores the meaning of the idea of family, this time by looking backwards in time at her own origins and speculating on the future of her own daughter.

The first verse introduces the candles as 'the last romantics' and takes up also in line 4 the religious imagery that will continue through the poem – 'grown milky, almost clear, like the bodies of saints'. The last line of that first verse leads on into the second verse, emphasising the words 'A whole family'. Five of the seven verses follow this same pattern: there is a break after line 4 and the final line continues into a sentence that is developed in the next verse. The structure of the poem mirrors the subject matter in this way and a sense of continuity is created. From the images of the first verse, the poem moves in the second verse to introduce 'the owner, past thirty, no beauty at all'. We are left to assume that this owner is the I-speaker of the third verse, though this is never stated directly. The third line of the third verse puts the speaker into context: 'This is no time for the private point of view'. Yet the privacy of memory cannot be ignored and the very next line 'When I light them, my nostrils prickle' is a prelude to recollections of a maternal grandmother from Vienna giving roses to Franz Josef and a grandfather in the Tyrol 'imagining himself a head waiter in America'. These recollections are prefaced, however, by the reference to the light of the candles that 'drag up false, Edwardian sentiments'. The past petrified by sentimentality is falsified and sterile.

The pattern of the final run-on line breaks after the moment in the poem when a direct link is made between maiden aunts and candles in the fifth verse:

> These little globes of light are sweet as pears.
> Kindly with invalids and mawkish women,
> They mollify the bald moon.

The Austrian relatives are part of another femininity, one condemned to sterility, to religious devotion, the antithesis of the bald moon that is the primeval White Goddess. They are 'non-souled', they 'never marry'. The I-speaker, contemplating her own child, reflects on how she will be perceived in the future:

> The eyes of the child I nurse are scarcely open.
> In twenty years I shall be retrograde
> As these draughty ephemerids.

The sixth verse ends like this, with a definite break. The final verse opens with a statement that continues the train of thought of the previous lines but is nevertheless quite separate. The continuity of perceptions of femininity within the family is being broken by the structure of the verse, even as the speaker asks her self-reflecting question:

> I watch their spilt tears cloud and dull to pearls.
> How shall I tell anything at all
> To this infant still in a birth-drowse?

And the poem ends with gentleness, with the shadow of these past, sterile women bending over the child, but with the mediating mother between them and the newborn's as yet undeveloped unconsciousness. The past cannot be denied access but it can be looked at with distance.

The image of the female relatives at a christening is the powerful first image of one of Plath's earlier poems, 'The Disquieting Muses', written in 1957. Discussing the poem on a BBC programme, Sylvia Plath commented:

> It borrows its title from a painting by Giorgio de Chirico – *The Disquieting Muses*. All through the poem I have in mind the enigmatic figures in this painting – three terrible faceless dressmaker's dummies in classical gowns, seated and standing in a weird, clear light that casts the long strong shadows characteristic of de Chirico's early work. The dummies suggest a twentieth-century version of other sinister trios of women – the Three Fates, the witches in *Macbeth*, De Quincey's sisters of madness.[6]

The mysterious women who appear 'nodding by night around my bed' are somehow the antithesis of the mother figure. The first verse is structured as a question to the mother and suggests that the recurring visitations by the three women are the mother's fault. The references here are to the story of Sleeping Beauty, whose parents unwisely did not invite the one female relative who caused the spell to be put upon the child. The second verse, still addressed to the mother, describes the way in which evil, ugly things had always been diluted by her:

> Mother, whose witches always, always
> Got baked into gingerbread

but asks the question whether the mother could in fact see and speak to the three women gathered round the child's bed.

The next three verses develop the theme of the mother's refusal to accept ugliness and unhappiness and her attempts to hide herself and her daughter from such things. In the third verse it is mother who offers cookies and Ovaltine and a comforting song to sing during a hurricane, in verse 4 it is mother who cries as her daughter stands 'heavy-footed', unable to lift a foot in 'the twinkle dress', while the other schoolgirls dance and sing; in the fifth verse it is mother who insists on piano lessons for her child and ignores the reports of every teacher that she is 'tone-deaf and yes, unteachable'. This verse ends with two lines that show the distance between the mother's vision of the world and the child's responses:

> I learned, I learned, I learned elsewhere,
> From muses unhired by you, dear mother.

The last two verses build on that distance. The sixth verse describes the mother floating 'in bluest air', an image used in 'The Moon and the Yew Tree' to describe the cold saints of Christianity, 'on a green balloon bright with a million/flowers and bluebirds that never were'. In contrast, the I-speaker's travelling companions are the three sinister, silent figures who cast shadows over her life. The last lines of the poem are enigmatic:

> And this is the kingdom you bore me to,
> Mother, mother. But no frown of mine
> Will betray the company I keep;

A striking feature of Sylvia Plath's letters to her mother is the cheerful tone, even at times when she must have been feeling desperately unhappy. But after her mother's visit in the summer of 1962, the mask of cheerfulness began to slip. In a letter of 21 October 1962, she wrote:

> Don't talk to me about the world needing cheerful stuff! What the person out of Belsen – physical or psychological – wants is nobody saying the birdies still go tweet-tweet, but the full knowledge that somebody else has been there and knows the *worst*, just what it is like. It is much more help for me, for example, to know that people are divorced and go through hell, than to hear about happy marriage. Let the *Ladies' Home Journal* blither about *those*.

The decision to maintain closeness with her mother on the levels that were available to them both seems to have been made at an early age. I do not think that there is any point in speculating about whether Sylvia Plath 'really' loved her mother or not. *The Bell Jar* documents Esther Greenwood's anger towards her mother, her resentment against the woman who tried too hard to live vicariously through her daughter's success, who wanted her daughter to have a secure, happy marriage. But the novel also acknowledges something else – that the problem is not so much Esther's aggressive feelings towards her mother and what that mother represents, rather it is her own inability to express those feelings, indeed until well into the book, to recognise that they are there.

The turning point comes in Chapter 16, when Esther dumps the dozen red roses brought by her mother as a birthday gift into the hospital wastebasket:

> That afternoon my mother had brought me the roses.
> 'Save them for my funeral', I'd said.
> My mother's face puckered, and she looked ready to cry.
> 'But Esther, don't you remember what day it is today?'
> 'No.'
> I thought it might be Saint Valentine's day.
> 'It's your *birth* day.'
> And that was when I had dumped the roses in the waste-basket.
> 'That was a silly thing for her to do', I said to Doctor Nolan.
> Doctor Nolan nodded. She seemed to know what I meant.
> 'I hate her', I said, and waited for the blow to fall.
> But Doctor Nolan only smiled at me as if something had pleased her very, very much, and said, 'I suppose you do'.[7]

Esther is on her way to recovery because she has acknowledged that part of her feeling for her mother is hatred. She is finally able to channel and direct that hatred outwards, instead of internalising it and directing it at herself.

In her *Journals* Sylvia Plath notes the complex range of feelings she has towards her mother:

> I may hate her, but that's not all. I... love her too. 'After all, as the story goes, she's my mother.' 'She can't encroach unless you're encroachable on.' So my hate and fear derive from my own insecurity. Which is? And how to combat it? (26 December 1958)

> WHAT DO I EXPECT BY 'LOVE' FROM HER? WHAT IS IT I DON'T GET THAT MAKES ME CRY? I think I have always felt she uses me as an extension of herself; that when I commit suicide, or try to, it is a 'shame' to her, an accusation: which it was, of course. (27 December 1958)

> One reason I could keep up such a satisfactory letter-relationship with her while in England was we could both verbalize our desired image of ourselves in relation to each other. (27 December 1958)

Going through analysis, as she was at this time, she had begun to tackle the problems between herself and her mother. Growing apart from her mother meant recognising that she too had tried to pretty over the feelings of anger and fear, in much the same way as her mother had done with her own life, and part of the process of self-knowledge meant taking those feelings out and looking at them. The same process also had to happen vis-à-vis her father and perhaps the emphasis she placed on this second relationship tended to over-shadow the problems with her mother up to that point in her life. Certainly, there are more poems about the father–daughter nexus than about the mother–daughter nexus, as if she had been more consciously aware of the need to work through the contradictory paternal relationship.

In her book, *Of Woman Born*, subtitled *Motherhood as Experience and Institution*, Adrienne Rich briefly mentions the relationship between Aurelia and Sylvia Plath in her chapter on motherhood and daugh-terhood. She notes the intensity of the letter-writing and comments that the mother–daughter relationship might be seen as the source of Sylvia Plath's early suicide attempt, her relentless perfectionism, and obsession with 'greatness'. Yet the preface to *Letters Home* reveals a remarkable woman, a true survivor; it was Plath's father who set the example of self-destructiveness.[8]

The importance of Adrienne Rich's book is that it puts the mother–child relationship into context, dealing openly with the darker side of that relationship. Reading it, the problems Sylvia Plath encountered with her own mother are not diminished but they are seen to be common to a good many women. That there was ambiguity in the relationship becomes, according to Rich, natural rather than unnatural. Although some critics have suggested that the complex negative feelings Sylvia Plath felt for her mother were a sign of her instability, such feelings can be shown to be simply part of the experience of a good many women, certainly of women belonging to that same generation. As Sylvia Plath married a foreigner, went to live abroad, gave up a steady career, moved out with a small child into the wilder-ness of a Devon village, became estranged from her husband, so all Aurelia Plath's value systems and hopes for her daughter's happiness (in the terms in which she construed that happiness) began to founder. Reading the poems, Journals and letters, it is hardly surprising that there should have been strong antagonistic feelings that surfaced. What is perhaps surprising is that there should still have been so much love and closeness between mother and daughter up to the end.

It is in her prose that Sylvia Plath deals primarily with the relationship with her mother. It is detailed in her *Journals*, it can be read through the letters home, together with Aurelia Plath's own text, it runs through some poems and, perhaps more than anywhere else, it provides a central motif for *The Bell Jar*. This novel, that was based on Sylvia Plath's own experiences when a student at Smith College and completed in 1961, details the breakdown and recovery of the symbolically named Esther Greenwood (Esther was a name that Sylvia Plath used more than once; the heroine of the story 'Mothers' is another Esther). Because it is so overtly autobiographical, it is tempting to read the novel on the same terms as the *Journals* or letters, leaving aside the fact that whereas the former texts were conceived of as intimate notes and letters consciously written for specific readers, the novel was clearly fiction. Reading that novel today, together with all the poems that are written in the first person, many critics have ignored the boundary line between writer and I-narrator and treated the literary texts on the same terms as the rest of Sylvia Plath's writings that are available to us. This tactic, it seems to me, is flawed, because it denies Sylvia Plath the credit of having been able to do the one thing she expressly wanted to do and that is to shape her experiences into art. A careful reading of the poems, for example, shows several I-speakers. There are different personae, who change from poem to poem. One of the last poems she wrote, 'Paralytic', dated 29 January 1963, has an I-narrator who talks about 'My wife, dead and flat, in 1920 pearls'. On the same day she wrote another poem entitled 'Gigolo', in which the I-speaker is again a man. Because her poems work on so many levels, there are layers of meaning that allow for the simultaneous presence of more than one speaker. So, when the speaker in 'Gigolo' says:

> And there is no end, no end of it.
> I shall never grow old. New oysters
> Shriek in the sea and I
> Glitter like Fontainebleau

The persona of the man preying on women coexists with an emblematic narcissist, 'tenderly' leaning over to look at his/her reflection in the water. The gigolo is present in the poem as a character, but the narcissism may or may not be one and the same with him.

Ted Hughes understands the dividing lines between autobiography and fiction in Sylvia Plath's writing and his preface to the *Johnny*

Panic collection, written in 1976, offers a way of reading her works that maintains and simultaneously deconstructs those barriers. Explaining why he has chosen, as editor, to select from her notebooks rather than to publish them in their entirety, Hughes says:

> It seems probable that her real creation was her own image, so that all her writings appear like notes and jottings directing attention towards that central problem – herself. Whether this is right or wrong, with some personalities it simply happened. As an editor of Sylvia Plath's unpublished writings, watching this happen to her, I am more and more inclined to think that any bit of evidence which corrects and clarifies our idea of what she really was is important, insofar as her writings persuade us of her importance. But living people figure everywhere even in her most private discussions with herself, and – an editor has to face it – some things are more important than revelations about writers. The vivid, cruel words she could use to pin down her acquaintances and even her close friends were nothing she would want published, and would be no joke to the recipients, still less so now that she is internationally famous and admired for her gift of phrase.[9]

He goes on to add, significantly 'This shouldn't need to be said'. That it did need to be said testifies to the problem of so much of Plath criticism that takes all her writings and reads them in the same way, that is, as documentary evidence about the 'truth' of her life and death and seeks to uncover more and more in the quest for that ultimate truth.

Although undoubtedly Sylvia Plath's relationship with her mother is explored in her writing, as is her relationship with her father, children, husband and the society of the age of the atomic bomb, so that exploration takes place within the framework of art forms. We can read *The Bell Jar* as a mother–daughter conflict novel, read the notes from the Journal, read Aurelia Plath's account of the joy and pain caused by her relationship with her daughter but the *way* to read these varied texts is as parts of the kaleidoscopic whole that is Sylvia Plath's life-work. Each piece of glass in a kaleidoscope contributes to the overall pattern; remove a piece and the pattern changes; shake up the parts and the pattern changes again. But there is no absolute final, true picture created by those glass particles, any more than there is a final, definitive, true self that the reader can uncover through reading a dead woman's brilliant, fragmentary papers.

Although she wrote the mother–daughter story primarily in prose, the father–daughter story occurs more frequently in poetry. One of the earliest father poems is 'On the Decline of Oracles' (1957) which has a direct reference to both the death of the father and to his German origins, two motifs that recur later on in the father poems. There is also a reference to the father as intellectual, another leitmotif of great prominence:

> My father died, and when he died
> He willed his books and shell away.
> The books burned up, sea took the shell,
> But I, I keep the voices he
> Set in my ear, and in my eye
> The sight of those blue, unseen waves
> For which the ghost of Böcklin grieves.

The poem that is perhaps most explicitly concerned with Sylvia Plath's working out of her relationship with her father is 'Electra on Azalea Path', written in March 1959. The inspirational source of the poem – a visit to her father's grave in Winthrop – is noted in her Journal, dated 9 March in the following terms:

Went to my father's grave, a very depressing sight. Three graveyards, separated by streets, all made within the last fifty years or so, crude, ugly block-stones, headstones together, as if the dead were sleeping head to head in a poorhouse. In the third yard, on a flat grassy area looking across a sallow barren stretch to rows of wooden tenements, I found the flat stone, 'Otto E. Plath: 1885–1940', right beside the path, where it would be walked over. Felt cheated. My temptation to dig him up. To prove he existed and really was dead. How far gone would he be? No trees, no peace, his headstone jammed up against the body on the other side. Left shortly. It is good to have the place in mind . . .

The same incident appears in *The Bell Jar*, when Esther goes to visit her father's grave, but here the tone is heavily ironic and the fictionalising process has transformed the experience into something consciously other:

The stones in the modern part were crude and cheap, and here and there a grave was rimmed with marble, like an oblong bathtub full of dirt, and rusty metal containers stuck up about where a person's navel would be, full of plastic flowers...

Then I saw my father's gravestone.

It was crowded right up by another gravestone, head to head, the way people are crowded in a charity ward when there isn't enough space. The stone was of a mottled pink marble, like tinned salmon, and all there was on it was my father's name and, under it, two dates, separated by a little dash.

At the foot of the stone I arranged the rainy armful of azaleas I had picked from a bush at the gateway of the graveyard. Then my legs folded under me, and I sat down in the sopping grass. I couldn't understand why I was crying so hard.

Then I remembered that I had never cried for my father's death.[10]

Two accounts of a visit to a father's grave, written by the same woman, but one written for herself and the other written as fiction and spoken by a protagonist whose search for emotional stability and self-knowledge provides the central theme of the book. Clearly the fictional version is linked to the notebook version but the 'reality' of the one text as opposed to the other cannot be determined. The one reality that *is* consistent, however, is the shaping force of the drive to come to terms with a dead father. In the Journal entry for 20 March in which she records the finishing of 'Electra on Azalea Path' together with the shorter 'Metaphors' a poem about pregnancy (the Journal records her concern for the possible bodily symptoms of pregnancy as a strong theme at this time), she writes about the problems of working through her father complex in analysis, noting that she does not feel that she is making much permanent progress: 'I may have all the answers to my questions in myself, but I need some catalyst to get them into my consciousness....' A month later, on 23 April, she rejects the Electra poem as 'too forced and rhetorical'.

'Electra on Azalea Path' is a poem of five stanzas, the first, third and fifth composed of ten lines, the second and fourth composed of eight lines, all with a rhyme on the first and last lines. Sylvia Plath borrows the Oresteia myth of Electra, the woman who waited for her father's homecoming, only to see him murdered by her mother and then waited again for her brother Orestes to come and avenge them both by killing their mother, Clytemnestra. The fourth stanza refers directly to this myth and refers also to the action that fuelled

Clytemnestra's hatred of her husband – the ritual murder of their daughter Iphigenia, Electra's sister, as a sacrifice to the gods to ensure a good wind for his warships en route to capture Troy. The figure of Electra is an ambiguous one – she appears both as victim and as hag, as avenger and as moral coward in various retellings of the story and it is this multiplicity that seems to dominate Sylvia Plath's poem, culminating in the final lines:

> O pardon the one who knocks for pardon at
> Your gate, father – your hound-bitch, daughter, friend.
> It was my love that did us both to death.

Above all, Electra is a woman who is torn between loyalties. Her desire for revenge against her mother, despite her knowledge of the source of her mother's hatred, isolates her from any kind of female solidarity. At the same time, her inability to act on her own behalf, without the strength of her brother Orestes, emphasises her weakness and non-masculinity. The Electra figure is an unhappy, marginalised outsider, doomed neither to share the confidence of her mother nor to enjoy the fruits of her loyalty to her father.

The very first line of the poem establishes the I-speaker's relationship to the dead father: 'The day you died I went into the dirt'. The speaker has been dead in her own way, dead to the awareness of her feelings for that father and the image developed through the first stanza is of bees, wintering in the 'lightless hibernaculum'. For twenty years, the poem suggests, the speaker has existed without the need for a father in a relationship with her mother:

> I had nothing to do with guilt or anything
> When I wormed back under my mother's heart.

The shorter second verse introduces another set of images and another stage in the developing relationship. The speaker is 'small as a doll' in her 'dress of innocence' and creates for herself a mythical figure, an epic story in which everything takes place 'in a durable whiteness'. But then there is a shift into Sylvia Plath's own autobiography and the ancient Greek Electra fuses with the contemporary one in four lines that describe the moment of awakening:

> The day I woke, I woke on Churchyard Hill
> I found your name, I found your bones and all

Enlisted in a cramped necropolis,
Your speckled stone askew by an iron fence.

The third stanza takes up the image of the charity ward, the poorhouse, to describe the crowded graveyard. Here also are the plastic flowers that do not rot but merely drip 'a bloody dye' in the rain. The last line of the third stanza leads on into the fourth:

The ersatz petals drip, and they drip red. (stanza 3)
Another kind of redness bothers me (stanza 4)

A technique of verse linkage that Sylvia Plath uses repeatedly throughout her poems. The fourth stanza changes the mood of the poem, for here the shift is both backwards in time again to the Greek myth, away from the New England churchyard and, significantly, towards some kind of female solidarity. Lines 2–4 are printed in italics:

The day your slack sail drank my sister's breath
The flat sea purpled like that evil cloth
My mother unrolled at your last homecoming.

The Electra-speaker of the poem seems here to be expressing her understanding at the causality of things – the father's ritual murder of the sister is linked to the moment of his death at the hands of his wife and the reference here is to the wine-red carpet that Clytemnestra unrolls before inviting Agamemnon to enter the house where he is murdered. But the association of redness and cloths carries connotations of menstrual blood; Electra, like her murdered sister and murdering mother, is a woman, a member of the opposite sex to her mysterious, lost father. The last four lines of the fourth stanza move on from this realisation, noting that 'the stilts of an old tragedy' are borrowed, that

The truth is, one late October, at my birth-cry
A scorpion stung its head, an ill-starred thing;

The I-speaker-Electra figure is marked for tragedy at birth. The fifth stanza relates bluntly the horror of the father's death, giving details that point towards a reference to Otto Plath:

> I brought my love to bear, and then you died.
> It was the gangrene ate you to the bone
> My mother said; you died like any man.

The daughter is left with the loss of the father to whom she had given her earliest love and with the words of the mother who explains in her own terms how he died. The ancient and modern Electras are again fused here, asked to trust the mother but seeking to know the father for themselves. The death of that father has killed off a part of the daughter too, and in the final lines of the poem, the I-speaker takes onto her own shoulders the burden for the father's death, the guilt that cannot be expiated. Electra has come full circle and admitted responsibility for having repressed and killed off the father whose idealised image she had tried to nurture.

The image of hibernating bees in the first stanza is linked to another father poem, written in 1957, 'The Beekeeper's Daughter'. The bee motif recurs throughout her verse, most importantly in a sequence of five poems written in the autumn of 1962 (see pp. 138–141). The bee is implicitly linked to her father, Otto Plath (author of a treatise on bumblebees), but at the same time it becomes a metaphor for sexual conflict. The powerful, ambiguous figure of the queen bee appears in 'The Beekeeper's Daughter' – 'Here is a queenship no mother can contest' – and is taken further in the later bee poems, written during another period of emotional crisis.

Within days of writing the later bee poems, Sylvia Plath wrote two poems, published in the *Collected Poems* as companion pieces, that deal head-on with savage anger towards both father and mother figures. 'Daddy', dated 12 October 1962, and 'Medusa', dated 16 October 1962, are poems for a father-figure and mother-figure respectively. They are strong, bitter poems, capable of being read on many levels simultaneously, and were written during the crisis days, when Ted Hughes moved out. Although the tone of the letters home is very different, some sense of the desperation she must have been feeling creeps into them. On 12 October in a letter to her brother Warren, she wrote that she was writing every day, from dawn until the children woke: 'a poem a day, and they are terrific'. On 16 October, writing to her mother, she says she is writing the best poems of her life that will make her name: 'I am a genius of a writer; I have it in me.' These two poems, which do indeed show great writing talent, bring together all kinds of sets of images linked to her writing about her mother and father and about sexual and marital conflicts.

In a reading for BBC radio of 'Daddy' Sylvia Plath explains:

> Here is a poem spoken by a girl with an Electra complex. Her father died while she thought he was God. Her case is complicated by that fact that her father was also a Nazi and her mother very possibly part Jewish. In the daughter the two strains marry and paralyse each other – she has to act out the awful little allegory once over before she is free of it.

'Daddy' is written in a powerful nursery rhyme rhythm that characterises several of the later poems. Here there are 16 verses of 5 lines each, with an irregular pattern of rhyme but with one dominant rhyme throughout. Forty-one of the 80 lines repeat the same rhyme: you/do/shoe/Jew/blue/screw and so on. The effect of this is to create an impression of great speed and furious energy, accentuated by the use of other devices – broken sentences, incomplete sentences, sentences without main verbs, repetition of certain words, use of German words. In the fourth and fifth verses the I-speaker claims she has had problems speaking:

> I never could talk to you.
> The tongue stuck in my jaw ...
> I could hardly speak.
> I thought every German was you.
> And the language obscene

As the poem progresses, the I-speaker becomes able to declare her feelings for her father, her hatred and fear for the figure who is depicted as Nazi, vampire, torturer and devil and gradually she comes to speak more clearly and coherently, in complete sentences at last. The twelfth verse gives details of her past relationship:

> I was ten when they buried you.
> At twenty I tried to die
> And get back, back, back to you.

But in the next verse comes the statement 'then I knew what to do'. The girl marries the image of her father, the 'man in black with a Meinkampf look/and a love of the rack and the screw;' but is finally able to reject him, to silence the voices that have prevented her from speaking. Husband and father, two in one, are the vampire which has drunk her blood for seven years (Sylvia Plath had married Ted Hughes in June 1956) and which she has now finally defeated:

> Daddy, you can lie back now.
> There's a stake in your fat black heart
> And the villagers never liked you.

The years of fear and pain are at an end, the evil male figure's reign of terror has been terminated by the stake through the heart. The poem ends with a maenad-like shriek of triumph, with the I-speaker feeling the solidarity of the villagers who had never liked her tormenter:

> They are dancing and stamping on you.
> They always *knew* it was you.
> Daddy, daddy, you bastard, I'm through.

The monstrous male figure of 'Daddy' has its female counterpart in 'Medusa'. In this poem, however, all the images are not so overtly universal as the Nazi or the vampire and some derive from Sylvia Plath's personal range of images linked to her mother – the de Chirico figures with their featureless heads and the hovering saints' effigies. The poem is made up of eight five-line verses and a single isolated last line, with no regular rhyme scheme or rhythmical pattern. What holds the poem together is the imagery, which writhes through it like the serpentine visions it arouses – flowing, hair, telephone cables, umbilical cords, tides and waves, fishing lines, a cobra and the central image of the jellyfish with its 'eely tentacle'. The mother-medusa, both sea-creature and gorgon and therefore able to inflict stinging pain and turn to stone in each manifestation respectively, comes uninvited into the world of the speaker:

> I didn't call you.
> I didn't call you at all.
> Nevertheless, nevertheless
> You steamed to me over the sea,
> Fat and red, a placenta
>
> Paralysing the kicking lovers.
> Cobra light

Squeezing the breath from the blood bells
Of the fuchsia. I could draw no breath.

The creature has come into her life, bridging the gap between them. But the I-speaker is perplexed by her relationship with the medusa and in the third verse asks 'Did I escape, I wonder', since her mind 'winds to you' and 'in any case, you are always there'. The umbilical relationship between daughter and mother-medusa binds them both together and the daughter cannot do anything except declare in the last line of the poem that 'there is nothing between us', which in view of what has gone before seems to be more of a wish or a hope than a statement.

'Medusa' provides a good example of the complexities of reading Sylvia Plath's poetry. Without biographical information (the poem expresses her resentment at what she saw as her mother's interference in her life), the poem becomes a surreal cry of horror at the invasion of the I-speaker's privacy by a monstrous thing, a creature of nightmare. We can assume the femaleness of the thing by the title and by the reference in the third verse to the umbilicus and in the seventh verse to 'Blubbery Mary', which also suggest connotations of motherhood. Other images remain unclear if the poem is taken out of context. But if it is read, as Ted Hughes suggests all her poems should be read, as part of a single work, then all sorts of references begin to make sense – the travelling over the sea, the religious imagery and, in the first verse, the 'God-ball' that is the head, recalling the imagery of that earlier mother poem, 'The Disquieting Muses'.

'Daddy' and 'Medusa' stand together as poems of great anger but also of great clarity. In both, the I-speaker explores the images of horror that face her and comes to the point of being able to take up a position of independence. After these poems the emphasis on the family in Sylvia Plath's writing seems to shift away from poems about mothers and fathers and towards poems about children. It is as if the stake through the heart of 'Daddy' and the cold final statement of 'Medusa' free something and many of the later poems explore the role of parenting from the point of view no longer of the child but of the adult. Just days after writing these two poems, she wrote 'By Candlelight' (24 October 1962) to her own baby son:

I hold my breath until you creak to life,
Balled hedgehog,
Small and cross.

followed by 'Nick and the Candlestick' (29 October 1962):

> You are the one
> Solid the spaces lean on, envious.
> You are the baby in the barn.

and one of her most beautiful lyrical poems, 'The Night Dances' (6 November 1962):

> Such pure leaps and spirals –
> Surely they travel
>
> The world forever, I shall not entirely
> Sit emptied of beauties, the gift
>
> Of your small breath, the drenched grass
> Smell of your sleeps, lilies, lilies.

The terrible sexual conflict of the father poems and the communication struggle of the mother poems is absent from these child-centred poems. Writing about herself as mother, there are moments of lyrical tranquility in some of Plath's poems. There may be 'a goddam baby screaming off somewhere' ('Stopped Dead') but there are also poems like 'Child', with its opening line:

> Your clear eye is the one absolutely beautiful thing.

5

Writing out Love

The poems written to her children reflect a passionate mother-love in the detailed beauty of imagery. The dead babies in glass jars have been transformed and the living babies are represented with love and tenderness:

> Love set you going like a fat gold watch.
> All night your moth-breath
> Flickers among the flat pink roses.
>
> 'Morning Song'

> I rock you like a boat
> Across the Indian carpet, the cold floor
>
> 'By Candlelight'

> Your clear eye is the one absolutely beautiful thing.
> I want to fill it with color and ducks,
> The zoo of the new
>
> 'Child'

> Your small
> Brother is making
> His balloon squeak like a cat.
> ...He bites,
> Then sits
> Back, fat jug
> Contemplating a world clear as water
>
> 'Balloons'

The poems to children have a directness about them that brings the reader in straight away to share the beauty of the picture. In these poems there seems to be no I-persona, no intermediary fictionalised figure that intervenes between the I-that-is-writer and the I-that-is-narrator within the poem. The mother who writes so powerfully

about her children is also the speaker and the poems are like love
letters to those children, messages without ambiguity.

The unambiguous nature of the love-poems to her children contrasts with the complex ambiguity of the poems about relationships
between men and women. In some of the very earliest poems Sylvia
Plath writes about love in intellectual terms; 'my love for you is
more/athletic than a verb' she writes in the second of her 'Trio of
Love Songs', or, at the end of the long, baroque 'Love is a Parallax',
'yet love/knows not of death nor calculus above/the simple sum of
heart plus heart'. These love poems are head poems, and in her
Journal she details her search for a man that she could love and live
with, in purely hypothetical terms. In an entry dated 27 April 1953,
she notes her fears of being left while 'everyone else is very married
and happy', her hopes for a soulmate that leave her disappointed if
she seizes on 'single symbols which supposedly presage large
assumptions' and comes to the conclusion that

> Let's face it, I am in danger of wanting my personal absolute to be
> a demigod of a man, and as there aren't many around, I often
> unconsciously manufacture my own. And then, I retreat and revel
> in poetry and literature where the reward value is tangible and
> accepted. I really do not think deeply, really deeply. I want a
> romantic non-existent hero.

Esther Greenwood in *The Bell Jar* also has ideas about some ideal
man. Instead she meets the boring, hypocritical all-American bour-
geois medic, Buddy Willard, the sadistic woman-hating Marco and
the stupid, incompetent Irwin with whom she loses her virginity.
Detailing that loss, Esther contrasts the symbolic significance of her
idealisation with the squalid reality of what took place:

> I lay, rapt and naked, on Irwin's rough blanket, waiting for the
> miraculous change to make itself felt.
>
> But all I felt was a sharp, startlingly bad pain.
> 'It hurts,' I said. 'Is it supposed to hurt?'
>
> Irwin didn't say anything. Then he said 'Sometimes it hurts'.[1]

Part of what Esther discovers about herself through the novel is to
value herself as a person, rather than as a set of constructed images,
designed to please someone else. She learns about expressing her

feelings, about coming to terms with negative emotions and she also learns about the mystification of sex and of male power. In her relationships with Buddy and with Marco, she can see that the men are far from perfect, indeed are totally inadequate for her needs, but she persists in trying to have a relationship with them simply because she thinks she needs a man in order to feel complete. Without a male partner, she would somehow be less than adequate. A similar line of thought runs through Sylvia Plath's early Journals and letters and shows how far she conformed to the dominant ideology of her time. Suzanne Juhasz describes the conflict between the mythical social woman and the alternative private woman in succinct terms:

> The exaggerated nature of her situation and suffering seems to have resulted from the peculiar temporal and social context in which Plath's life and art grew: the fifties, New England, the middle class. Sylvia Plath as high school and college super achiever, the prettiest, the most popular, *and* the smartest, with her dark-red lipsticked smile, her carefully waved hair, a perfection of surfaces, was in discord with another 'self': the poet whose words could destroy surfaces and open inner places, inner wounds, inner emptiness.[2]

The woman writing villanelles in her college days was to write very differently about love and about men in her later poems. One of her strongest, most bitterly feminist poems is 'The Applicant', dated 11 October 1962. Introducing this poem for a BBC radio reading, Sylvia Plath describes the I-speaker as 'an executive, a sort of exacting supersalesman', who wants to be sure that 'the applicant for his marvellous product really needs it and will treat it right'. The poem is structured as an interview in eight verses. The salesman questions the applicant and only gradually does the reader discover what it is that the applicant is being offered: a wife. In the last verse the salesman refers to the applicant as 'my boy', a phrase that explicitly reinforces the bond of maleness that exists between them.

The first verse opens with a question: 'First, are you our sort of person?' and moves straight into the surreal with a list of physical props that the applicant might be wearing, 'a glass eye, false teeth or a crutch/ a brace or hook/rubber breasts or a rubber crotch'. When he learns that none of these are needed, the salesman changes tactics. The applicant does not need a physical prop but he is crying and his hand, when asked to hold it out, is empty. The salesman offers his merchandise:

> Here is a hand
> To fill it and willing
> To bring teacups and roll away headaches
> And do whatever you tell it.

If he marries this 'it' (the wife is never referred to as 'she' but always as 'it') 'it' is guaranteed to stay until death – 'to thumb shut your eyes at the end/and dissolve of sorrow'.

Then the salesman tries another line of patter. 'I notice you are stark naked', he says, offering a black suit that is 'waterproof, shatterproof, proof/against fire and bombs through the roof'. Marriage for the applicant will be an insurance, a protection forever against unpleasant things. In the sixth verse the salesman notes that the applicant's head 'is empty', but that this need be no problem. He summons the wife-figure out of the closet and offers her for inspection:

> Naked as paper to start
> But in twenty-five years she'll be silver,
> In fifty, gold.
> A living doll, everywhere you look.

In the last two verses, the salesman's patter speeds up, through the use of rhyme and repetition, into a finale of intense bitterness. The applicant cannot afford to miss this great opportunity. The wife will do everything for him:

> It can sew, it can cook,
> It can talk, talk, talk.

The wife comes in full working order and will complement the applicant in every possible way; 'You have a hole, it's a poultice/ you have an eye, it's an image'. The applicant cannot refuse:

> My boy, it's your last resort.
> Will you marry it, marry it, marry it.

This is a heavily ironic poem in which the speaker expresses total contempt for marriage and for women. The wife is nothing but an instrument for the husband's use, an object to care for him, console him, do his every bidding. She has no mind of her own, no will of her own. She is even desexed to the point of being an 'it'. The only relationship within the poem is the purely commercial one between salesman and applicant and the world they inhabit is one in which men are supreme. Women are reduced to a function, they exist as robots for men's use, as suits of clothes, no more.

Ten days later, Plath wrote 'Lyonnesse', a poem dealing with the loss of idealism. This poem is made up of nine short verses of three lines each and the narrative consists of a series of images, presented in the third person. The first line sets the tone of the poem and establishes the main line through: 'No use whistling for Lyonnesse'. The kingdom, if it ever existed, has vanished under the sea. Already in Arthurian legend the kingdom of Lyonnesse was a mythical, ideal place off the coast of Cornwall. Here it is used as a symbol for something beautiful and lost that can never be recovered. The second line establishes another image: 'Sea-cold, sea-cold it certainly is' and the third line introduces the 'he' that is the 'big God' of the last three verses of the poem. Lyonnesse has sunk into him and what remains is

> The blue, green,
> Gray, indeterminate gilt
> Sea of his eyes washing over it

The lost land under the sea and the male figure are fused in the imagery of this poem. Again it is a poem that can be read on several levels but which offers the widest range of readings if taken in context and read as a part of Sylvia Plath's total work. There are echoes in this poem of the 1956 poem to Ted Hughes, 'Letter to a Purist', where the beloved is described as being greater than

> That grandiose colossus who
> Stood astride
> The envious assaults of sea
> (Essaying, wave by wave,
> Tide by tide,
> To undo him, perpetually)

The beloved is contrasted with the colossus who holds back the sea; whereas in 'Lyonnesse' the huge male figure no longer has such power. The land with all its people has slipped under the sea and continues unknowingly in that new world:

> The clear, green, quite breathable atmosphere,
> Cold grits underfoot,
> And the spidery water-dazzle on field and street.

The 'big God' has allowed this to happen, he has 'lazily closed one eye and let them slip'; Lyonnesse and its people and cows are no longer protected by him.

The last five lines of the poem change the emphasis of what has gone before. The lost land with all its beauty, the God's neglect, the swirl of the sea over dreams of happiness are narrated in the third person, with impersonal sentence constructions adding to the effect of distance from emotion. In the last five lines the viewpoint shifts from the people and the land to the god-figure:

> They did not see him smile,
> Turn, like an animal,
> In his cage of ether, his cage of stars.

The god-figure is trapped, beast-like, in a cage made by his very existence. The penultimate line offers an ironic excuse – 'He'd had so many wars', which is then undercut by the savage thrust of the final line – 'The white gape of his mind was the real Tabula Rasa'. There is nothing in the god's mind, he is a void within himself and therefore his irresponsibility is part of his make-up. The Tabula Rasa contrasts ironically with the idea of the Round Table, symbol of knighthood and perfection. This male god-figure is a sterile, white hole.

The sadness of loss that pervades 'Lyonnesse' is accentuated by the echoes of the early love poetry that Sylvia Plath wrote in the first months of passion for Ted Hughes. 'Ode for Ted' is an exuberant, elaborate poem that portrays Ted Hughes as a kind of nature god, a figure who can command obedience from the earth and the animal kingdom. He is another Adam, and the woman who loves him is not even given a name, simply referred to as 'this Adam's woman', an appendage to his greatness. Sending this poem to her mother, together with another entitled 'Song' in a letter dated 21 April 1956, Sylvia Plath writes that the poems are meant to be said aloud 'and they are from my joy in discovering a world I never knew: all nature'. Two days earlier, in another letter to her mother, she had written:

I shall tell you now about something most miraculous and thundering and terrifying and wish you to think on it and share some of it. It is this man, this poet, this Ted Hughes. I have never known anything like it. For the first time in my life I can use *all* my knowing and laughing and force and writing to the hilt all the time, everything, and you should see him, hear him!

He has a health and hugeness...the more he writes poems, the more he writes poems. He knows all about the habits of animals and takes me amid cows and coots. I am writing poems and they are better and stronger than anything I have ever done...Daily I am full of poems; my joy whirls in tongues of words...I feel a growing strength. I do not merely idolize, I see right into the core of him.

And so the poems came, with the image of the larger-than-life man running through them – the god of nature, the colossus, the faun, with the narrator of these poems watching, observing this great male figure rather than participating with him on equal terms. The last two lines of 'Faun' are typical of this narrative stance:

> Marked how god rose
> And galloped woodward in that guise.

In another poem, 'Pursuit', which is steeped in sexually symbolic imagery, the narrator is fleeing from a panther, a 'black marauder, hauled by love/on fluent haunches' which will not let her escape.

Margaret Uroff has compared some of the poems from this period with Ted Hughes' poems written at the same time and comes to the conclusion that 'Hughes' poetic presence' is very strongly there in Sylvia Plath's writing, through the use of nature imagery, 'the claws, beaks, blood and marauders'.[3] Hughes, she claims, helped Sylvia Plath free herself from the forms she had been using, from the villanelle and the sonnet, showing her how to work in strongly stressed syllabic patterns. But she also argues that Hughes' work shows evidence of Sylvia Plath's influence and claims further that both writers sound like Yeats. Sylvia Plath's letters show the importance that both attached to reading and studying writing together in the early stages of their relationship, so the mutual influence is hardly surprising. But one feature that emerges strongly from the early love poems is the passivity of the female, who, despite the energetic language of the verse, is cast in the role of priestess worshipping and tending the godhead.

Sylvia Plath's emphasis on Ted Hughes' strength, both physical and intellectual, on his power over women and animals, on his apparently superhuman ability to commune with the world of nature has sometimes troubled critics who perceive the ideological dangers of such adulation. Judith Kroll comments that 'the excessive glorification of her husband is discomfortingly redolent of fascist sensibility',[4] adding that it is not surprising that the husband/father figure should eventually appear in the poetry as a Nazi, since

> he was originally worshipped as a (fascist) god, as an ideal of adolescent longing.

In an entry in the Journal for March 1958, Sylvia Plath writes about her feelings for her husband, in terms of self-effacement:

> I am, at bottom, simple, credulous, feminine and loving to be mastered, cared-for

but adds a rider to this apparently submissive statement:

> but I will kill with my mind, my ice-eye, anyone who is weak, false, sickly in soul.

Ted Hughes, she writes, uses all of her and this use inspires her to love and to give with no fear of 'lies, misuse, betrayal'. The very insistence on the perfection of their love, the repetition in the Journal and the letters of superlatives seems almost to speak of what she *hoped* might be, rather than what she was recording as extant. In this same Journal entry there is a sentence that reads like a prayer for the success of her relationship with Ted:

> May my demons and seraphs guard me on the right way and may we live long toward white hair and creative wisdom and die in a flash of light in each other's arms.

But Sylvia Plath's husband-worship is by no means total nor is her attitude to him unambiguous. What comes across from the poems and Journal entries is her love for him, her exuberance, her joy in discovering things in herself that she had not realised before. And having found an ideal figure to love and be loved by, she records in her writing great swings from the lavishly hypothetical to the down-to-earth practical. Having balked for so long at the idea of marrying a man and washing his socks, she seems surprised at the way in which domesticity and creativity fuse in her life, causing a certain hitherto inexperienced, though not unpleasant, tension. A few lines further on from her prayer to her demons and seraphs, she records how she carefully 'filled Ted's slippers with a chocolate rabbit and ten tiny chocolate eggs', adding 'I believe he has eaten them all'. She seems to have been trying to balance a range of different needs and different idealisations with the preconceptions about marriage and about men that she had previously seen as central to her life. Principal among these conflicting impulses was the fact that in her relationship with Ted Hughes the old division between marriage and career seemed to have been abolished. Here was a person with whom she could live as wife and coexist as fellow writer. Esther Greenwood's dilemma appeared to have been solved. The next hurdle to be over-come was what she described in a letter to her mother of 13 November 1956 as 'the ingrained English maxim that a woman cannot cook and think at the same time'.

Despite the joy she expressed in her letters, she published a story in 1957, 'The Wishing Box', that is based on the gap between reality and an ideal of marital happiness. Harold and Agnes are a married couple living in a comfortable American suburban house. Over breakfast, Harold tells Agnes about his dreams and as the weeks pass Agnes comes to bitterly resent the lavishly coloured exciting world of Harold's dreams, a world that she feels excluded from. Her dreams, which she keeps to herself, are dark and ominous, she has left the dreams of 'a wishing box land above the clouds where wishing boxes grew on trees' behind her in her childhood. Finally she confesses to Harold that she does not dream any more and Harold tries to teach her to dream, showing her the way how. 'Perhaps you just don't use your powers of imagination enough', he tells her patronis-ingly. Agnes tries to help herself by reading anything she can lay her hands on, then by watching TV, finally by drinking sherry. The story ends with Harold returning home from work to find Agnes lying on the living-room sofa

dressed in her favourite princess-style emerald taffeta evening gown, pale and lovely as a blown lily, eyes shut, an empty pillbox and an overturned water tumbler on the rug at her side. Her tranquil features were set in a slight, secret smile of triumph, as if, in some far country unattainable to mortal men, she were, at last, waltzing with the dark, red-caped prince of her early dreams.[5]

The boring reality of life as a suburban housewife proves too much for Agnes. She dies, and her death is ambiguous. The reader is left to decide whether she deliberately chose to put an end to the boredom of her life, or whether she tried somehow to enter the world of dreams and fantasy. Sadie, the frustrated wife in another short story, 'The Fifty-ninth Bear', published in 1961 does not kill herself to escape her husband. Instead, the power of her will summons up the creature that kills him. In the final lines of the story, Norton, the husband, goes to investigate what the bear is doing outside their tent late at night:

He held the light steady, moving forward, willing the bear to be gone. At any moment the bear should break and run. 'Get out...' But there was another will working, a will stronger, even, than his.

The darkness fisted and struck. The light went out. The moon went out in a cloud. A hot nausea flared through his heart and bowels. He struggled, tasting the thick, sweet honey that filled his throat and oozed from his nostrils. As from a far and rapidly receding planet, he heard a shrill cry – of terror, or triumph, he could not tell.

It was the last bear, her bear, the fifty-ninth.[6]

In her Journal entry for 17 December 1958, Sylvia Plath outlines an idea for another story, about an 'advanced' couple, without children, in which the woman had a career and the two are 'above sewing on buttons, cooking'. The problems start when the husband demurs:

The husband thinks he agrees, fight over sewing on buttons. Not really fight about that. Fight about his deep-rooted conventional ideas of womanhood, like all the rest of the men, wants them pregnant and in the kitchen. Wants to shame her in public; told from point of view of wise elderly matron? advice? ah, what is it?

The same Journal entry details quarrels with Ted Hughes about just such issues as sewing on buttons. She notes that when he wants to 'manipulate' her, he tells her she is like her mother. This was the period of Sylvia Plath's sessions with an analyst, during which she had begun to investigate her feelings for her parents, her sense of loss and anger over her father and her love–hate relationship with her mother. What also emerges from the pages of the notebooks is her ambiguity towards her husband; not in the sense of declining love for him but in terms of dealing with him as less than the ideal-ised figure of her imagination. On 26 December she notes that 'I do fight with Ted', mainly over money. She also records her jealousy of him, her dreams about him leaving her for other women. On 27 December, she records just such a dream,

> I dreamed the other night of running after Ted through a huge hospital, knowing he was with another woman, going into mad wards and looking for him everywhere: what makes you think it was Ted? It had his face but it was my father, my mother.

Living with a husband, even a good one, was by no means the fairy-tale happy-ever-after promised to Cinderella and Snow White, particularly for a woman who wanted everything – happy marriage, career, success, fame, children and the physical time in which to write.

In February 1961, after her miscarriage, Sylvia Plath wrote a deeply troubled poem, 'Zoo Keeper's Wife'. This poem, made up of five eight-line stanzas, traces the causes of the Zoo Keeper's Wife's sleeplessness through a series of disturbing animal images. The I-speaker addresses herself to 'you', the husband, who wooed her 'with the wolf-headed fruit bats/hanging from their scorched hooks in the moist/fug of the Small Mammal House'. There is no explicit accusation levelled at him but the implicit accusations run through the language of the poem, most pointedly in the last line of each verse.

The poem opens with an aggressive statement: 'I can stay awake all night, if need be', and switches immediately into a chain of images. She is 'cold as an eel, without eyelids' and the darkness around her is 'a dead lake', 'a spectacular plum fruit'. After these images of coldness and stasis, the next four lines go beyond recognisable shapes. 'I am lungless/and ugly', says the I-speaker, 'my belly a silk stocking'. Neither human nor fish, she is a shapeless thing in the darkness, though linked to other females, since in her belly 'the heads and tails of my sisters decompose'. The last line of this verse invites the reader to look at that process of decomposition – 'they are melting like coins in the powerful juices'. Her belly, which ought to bring forth life, is the source of death and destruction.

The primeval imagery of the first verse gives way in the second to another stage of development, 'the spidery jaws, the spine bones' of fossil creatures with backbones. Each verse of this poem has imagery which relates to a stage of human development, from the amoeba to the ape and to man with his Tree of Knowledge. But into the second verse comes another line of thought – 'Old grievances, jostling each other', in the second line, which leads on straight away to a direct address to her husband:

> But what do you know about that
> My fat pork, my marrowy sweetheart, face-to-the-wall?
> Some things of the world are indigestible.

The third verse recalls his courtship in the zoo and images of nega-tivity increase. The fruit bats are 'wolf-headed', the armadillo is 'obscene and bald as a pig', the white mice are 'multiplied to infinity like angels on a pinhead/out of sheer boredom'. As she comes back to her present state of sleeplessness, 'tangled in the sweat-wet sheets', she recalls 'the bloodied chicks and the quartered rabbits'. Images of death predominate over images of nourishment.

In the fourth verse, the Zoo Keeper's Wife recounts how she responded to his courtship by pretending to be the Tree of Know-ledge, by entering his bible, by boarding his ark. The religious sym-bolism carries connotations of the Adam and Eve story but the key word 'pretended' underlines the lack of communication between the two. The last line of the fourth verse leads on into the fifth: 'I can't get it out of my mind/how our courtship lit the tindery cages'. But the animal imagery takes on new dimensions of horror; the mouth of the rhinoceros is 'dirty as a bootsole and big as a hospital sink', the creature has 'bog-breath'. Snails blow 'kisses like black apples'. The associations of kissing with the sliminess of the snails effectively deconstructs any ideas of tenderness or passion. The last two lines return us to the start of the poem, to the wife's sleeplessness:

> Nightly now I flog apes owls bears sheep
> Over their iron stile. And still don't sleep.

There are several narrative lines running through this poem – the history of the development of mankind from its origins in the primeval swamp, the growth of a foetus and the associations of untimely end through the image of bloodied chicks and quartered rabbits, the uselessness of knowledge, religion and medicine (seen as belonging to the husband, the male) as a means of helping the wife to a cure and, finally, the sinister wooing of the zookeeper whose wife lies sleepless and troubled, beyond his understanding. She lies in bed, turning over in her mind these images of ugliness and death, whilst he lies, face to the wall, a piece of fat pork.

In May 1962 Sylvia Plath wrote 'Event', another poem with a central motif of a husband and wife lying in bed together, separated by pain. The I-speaker of this poem does not have any specific persona, she is simply wife and mother and suffering human being. In contrast to the concrete animal imagery of 'Zoo Keeper's Wife', 'Event' combines more abstract images with occasional terrifyingly concrete images, like the 'small white maggot' of the soul that symbolises loneliness and decomposition. The poem is made up of seven three-line verses and a single last line. It opens with an exclamation – 'How the elements solidify!' and qualifies that sentence with an image in the next line of moonlight as a chalk cliff, 'in whose rift we lie/back to back'. All softness has turned hard, moonlight is rock, words become 'intolerable vowels' and pierce the heart, the face of the baby in the nearby crib is 'carved in pained, red wood'. Even the stars are hard. The only softness is the small white maggot, image of putrefaction.

Each of the first four verses of the poem moves in space, from the moonlight and the owl outside the window to the bed, then to the crib, back outside to the night sky. In the fourth verse there is a sudden movement – 'One touch', but this 'burns and sickens'. It cannot soften the hard textures. The fifth verse develops a new image and a new stage in the narrative – the iciness of apple blossom, symbol of love and weddings, and the ring 'a groove of old faults, deep and bitter'. This is a marriage which has turned to stone. In the next verse that is made explicit:

> Love cannot come here.
> A black gap discloses itself.

The maggot-soul (and there is a deliberate reference here to the dainty, fleeting, joyous little soul of the Emperor Hadrian's famous poem) is on the opposite lip of the divide. The I-speaker is disintegrating – 'My limbs, also, have left me'. In the penultimate line she asks the question that refers both to the lost limbs and to the separated couple: 'Who has dismembered us?' The poem ends with a note of despair: 'The dark is melting. We touch like cripples'. All possibility of wholeness and unity has gone.

As her marriage collapsed, Sylvia Plath's poetry about domestic crisis increased in output. The gap between biography and creative output is very narrow here and the poems can be read as a kind of diary. 'Words heard, by accident, over the phone', dated 11 July 1962, is built around the image of the telephone as a monstrous tentacled alien thing that pours mud, excrement and spawn into the speaker's life. 'Burning the Letters', dated 13 August 1962, compares the pain of this destruction to dogs tearing a fox to pieces; 'For a Fatherless Son', dated 26 September 1962, uses the image of a dead tree in the Australian outback to describe the loss of the father that the child has not yet understood; 'The Courage of Shutting-Up', dated 2 October 1962, is full of imagery of battle between nations. The speed with which these poems must have been written shows the extent of the energy flow behind them. In his notes on the chronological order of her poems, Ted Hughes describes how her method of writing had changed with the writing of 'Tulips', dated 18 March 1961:

> The two years between 1960 and 1962 had produced some beautiful poems, but only three that she selected for *Ariel*. She had heard what her real voice sounded like, and now had a new standard for herself. The poem called TULIPS was the first sign of what was on its way. She wrote this poem without her usual studies over the Thesaurus, and at top speed, as one might write an urgent letter. From then on, all her poems were written in this way.[7]

The poems of domestic crisis reach a kind of climax in 'Lesbos' (18 October 1962), a long poem in free verse made up of irregular sections and a single last line. The title of the poem is ironic; Lesbos was the centre of female intellectual activity in ancient Greece, presided over by the poet Sappho, but here it is used to indicate both the common experience of suffering at the hands of men that women share and the failure of the two women in the poem to communicate with one another and help lessen the pain.

The crucial underpinning structure in the poem is the pattern of sound. Sylvia Plath's carefully crafted earlier poems had given way to other kinds of structuring, most notably the patterning of sounds. These poems, after all, were written to be read aloud. The dominant sounds in 'Lesbos' are s/z sounds that create an effect of hissing, of breath being held back and escaping through clenched teeth. The first lines of the poem set the scene and establish this sound pattern:

> Viciousness in the kitchen!
> The potatoes hiss.
> It is all Hollywood, windowless,
> The fluorescent light wincing on and off like a terrible migraine

The I-speaker's two-year-old daughter is having a tantrum, screaming 'facedown on the floor', their hostess, the 'you' of the poem has put the child's kittens outside the door 'where they crap and puke and cry and she can't hear', a 'fat snail' of a baby sits on the linoleum, there is 'a stink of fat and baby crap' and the hostess' 'impotent husband slumps out for a coffee'. In this hellish scene (and the poem uses a series of images of hell, with references to smog and sparks and the moon that 'dragged its blood bag' like a 'sick animal') the two women are locked in conflict. Through the first section of the poem the I-speaker recounts with bitter irony the advice given to her by the 'you' – and the ludicrously rhymed lines with their references to T. S. Eliot express the I-speaker's point of view:

> I should sit on a rock off Cornwall and comb my hair.
> I should wear tiger pants, I should have an affair.
> We should meet in another life, we should meet in air,
> Me and you.

This first section sets out the difference between the two women through the use of pronouns. The sentences that open with 'you say' become progressively more outrageous as the I-speaker details the hatred of women that her hostess reveals:

> You say you can't stand her,
> The bastard's a girl....
> You say I should drown the kittens. Their smell!
> You say I should drown my girl....
> The baby smiles.../You could eat him. He's a boy.
> You say your husband is just no good to you.
> His Jew-Mama guards his sweet sex like a pearl.

The next section of the poem moves into nostalgia. The You-woman recalls her past life, when she was beautiful and adored by men in New York and Hollywood. The images of hell proliferate, the hatred between the two women turns inward until there is silence between them:

> Now I am silent, hate
> Up to my neck,
> Thick, thick.
> I do not speak.

The I-speaker packs her belongings, her cats and her children. 'O vase of acid' is her description of the other woman, 'You know who you hate'. But although that hatred is outwardly directed towards other women, the I-speaker sees that the real object of hatred is the husband who 'is hugging his ball and chain down by the gate'. As she leaves, uttering polite platitudes, she shares a moment of contact with the other woman. Both are bound together in a recognition of the meaning of lies:

> I say I may be back.
> You know what lies are for.
> Even in your Zen heaven we shan't meet.

There is no Lesbos here, no communication between these two women who ought to be united in their misery. They come from different worlds and the You-woman has denied the bond that ought to have linked her to others. She adores male children even while loathing the male adult with whom she lives, she discriminates against the female child, she has blown her tubes 'like a bad radio/ clear of voices and history'.

The poems after 'Lesbos' continue to develop the themes of crisis in relationships and the loss of love but they move outwards again in subject matter, through the use of dramatic personae, further away from detailing the intimate biography of Sylvia Plath's daily life. For me, reading these poems, there is a striking sense of the writer having entered a new phase. Despite the pain in the language, there is another element – an emphasis on fighting back rather than sinking down under the weight of it all. Some of the beautiful lyrical poems to children show an awareness of the joy that was still possible despite the suffering and in other poems there are references to resurrection.

Two poems written within days of each other at the end of October 1962, 'Purdah' and 'Lady Lazarus', both develop this idea of the woman who transcends her torments and exacts revenge for her suffering on men. 'Purdah' is made up of nineteen short three-line verses, some of which consist of a single word. This carefully minimised language combines with the content material of the poem to create an image of a woman who is contained, both within the walls of the building in which she has been placed by her bridegroom and within the boundaries of her own consciousness. The woman has been reduced to an object, a statuette:

> Jade –
> Stone of the side,
> The agonized
> Side of green Adam, I
> Smile, cross-legged,
> Enigmatical,
> Shifting my clarities.

She is her master's possession, denied the right to speak and move freely, and the tense, abbreviated language of the poem gives the reader a physical impression of restriction. But within the structure, there are developing patterns that show movement within: words are repeated – 'mirror', 'attendants', 'one' – and again the sound pattern of sibilants hisses through the poem. The woman behind the veil, 'priceless and quiet' is breathing and 'the mouth/veil stirs its curtains', she watches and her 'eye/veil is/a concatenation of rainbows'. In the thirteenth verse the woman utters for the first time the phrase that she will use three times more: 'I shall unloose'. First, she will unloose 'one feather, like the peacock', then 'one note/ shattering the chandelier/of air'. Then finally comes the moment of total release, prefigured by the double repetition of the phrase 'I shall unloose': what will be unloosed from 'the small jeweled doll he guards like a heart' is his destruction

> The lioness,
> The shriek in the bath,
> The cloak of holes.

The lioness, symbol of female strength, will be unleashed against him. The last two lines carry connotations of other moments of female revenge – the murder of Marat in his bath by Charlotte Corday, the stabbing of Agamemnon by his wronged wife Clytemnestra. The beloved doll beneath her veils harbours murder in her heart.

The tone of 'Lady Lazarus' is very different but the final point made is similar. The I-speaker, whose language is the brittle, acidly comic language of a female Lenny Bruce, presents her act to the public:

> It's the theatrical
>
> Comeback in broad day
> To the same place, the same face, the same brute
> Amused shout:
>
> 'A miracle!'
> That knocks me out.

The 'peanut-crunching crowd' that shoves in to see her resurrection wants a show but she tells them that this time they will have to pay 'a very large charge' for it. She is 'only thirty' and 'like the cat I have nine times to die', but this is her third resurrection:

> The first time it happened I was ten.
> It was an accident.
>
> The second time I meant
> To last it out and not come back at all.

In the first lines of the poem, the I-speaker boasts about her ability to keep coming back:

> I have done it again.
>
> One year in every ten
> I manage it –

But she has come back once again into the world of male savagery. Her impresario is a Nazi:

> So, so, Herr Doktor.
> So, Herr Enemy.

> I am your opus,
> I am your valuable.

She describes herself in terms of a concentration camp victim of that monstrous figure – 'my skin/bright as a Nazi lampshade', 'my face a featureless, fine/Jew linen'. Burned to ashes, flesh and bone dissolve. All that is left are the objects that would not burn, like the gold filling or wedding ring and the cake of soap, made with melted body fat.

But despite this horrific image of her destruction, Lady Lazarus is not finished yet. She has come back before and will come back again. The last lines of the poem are a warning to all men and to the system of male values that sets even a male god above all. God and Lucifer are both addressed as 'Herr', in a deliberate attempt to emphasise their common male-ness:

> Herr God, Herr Lucifer
> Beware
> Beware.
>
> Out of the ash
> I rise with my red hair
> And I eat men like air.

Introducing this poem for BBC radio, Sylvia Plath said:

> The speaker is a woman who has the great and terrible gift of being reborn. The only trouble is, she has to die first. She is the Phoenix, the libertarian spirit, what you will. She is also just a good, plain resourceful woman.

Lady Lazarus is a survivor, a woman who understands the nature of her enemy and returns to fight back.

The anger of the fighting back poems is directed against men who wrong women and against the world which stands by and allows them to do it. After 'Lady Lazarus', there is another change in the poems, as if the phase of rage had come to an end. Love is still a theme in several poems but that love is no longer presented as linked to conflict, rather to profound sadness. It is as if the anger poems represent a journey through hell and the quieter poems represent the arrival on the shores of purgatory. Dante, after struggling past Lucifer himself, came out onto the shores of pearly solitude

that marked the beginning of his journey towards Mount Purgatory.
Since Sylvia Plath's poems are full of literary references of all kinds,
encoded into the language, the parallel with Dante is not so far-
fetched. Dante's journey through hell and on through purgatory
towards paradise has become an archetype of western literary culture.

'The Couriers', dated 4 November 1962, is a deeply sad poem. It
consists of six two-line verses and a single last line and the first three
couplets are written as question and answer. The three questions
introduce three distinct images. The first is surrealistic – 'the word of
a snail on the plate of a leaf', the second is impossible – 'acetic acid in
a scaled tin' and the third, which ought to be possible is therefore
made impossible by being offered after the other two – 'a ring of
gold with the sun in it'. The answer to the first two questions is in
the negative and the phrase 'do not accept it' is repeated in each. But
the answer to the question about the ring and the sun comes in five
words, without a main verb: 'Lies. Lies and a grief'. The ring of gold,
symbol of weddings, of perfection, of power and resolution, is nothing
but lies and a grief.

The three questions carry connotations of myth and fairy tale with
them. Heroes on a quest are frequently given three tasks to fulfil,
three questions to answer. In Celtic legend those questions may be
put to the three fates, the women tending the cauldron which, in
Welsh romance, was a cauldron of inspiration and knowledge,
prepared by Cerridwen, a manifestation of the White Goddess. The
cauldron in this poem is clearly female-created, described as 'immacu-
late' (the adjective used to describe the Virgin Mary). It is a cauldron
that is one and many, since it is 'talking and crackling/all to itself on
the top of each/on nine black Alps'. Nine is another sacred female
number and there may be connotations in the image of the nine
peaks of the Aroanian mountains, above Nonacris (city of 'nine
heights') where the daughters of Proteus are supposed to have gone
when overtaken by madness. Graves gives details of this legend and
tells how those same women were eventually found and healed of
their madness through secret rites.[8]

The three riddles of the first three couplets are answered nega-
tively. In the second section of the poem various strands of mythology
are fused together – the cauldron of Celtic legend, the Daughters of
Proteus of Greek legend and, through the reference to 'a disturbance
of mirrors', perhaps also the bewitched Lady of Shallott of Arthurian
romance. What is significant about these legends is that they are all
concerned with women breaking spells or exercising their power.

And that power stretches up into mountains and out across seas and into the very fabric of time itself. The last line of the poem is a kind of incantation – 'Love, love, my season'. Love is part of the changing year, everywhere and yet nowhere permanently. The message of the couriers is a sad one; the absence of living people in this poem, the enigmatic questions and answers are beyond pain. The 'disturbance in mirrors', with the 'sea shattering its gray one' is an image that echoes through several of the poems from this period and recalls to mind the 'blue, green/gray, indeterminate gilt/sea' of the eyes of the god-figure in 'Lyonnesse'. Although love is named in the last line of the poem, it exists in the rest of the poem as an absence not as a presence. It is as remote as the Holy Grail.

The poems from November 1962 onwards are full of complex patterns of references taken from Sylvia Plath's own life and previous writings, from classical mythology and Celtic mythology, from other literary sources and from religion. Through this densely woven web of references the poems move outwards and take on a universality that makes them so extraordinary. The common critical appellage of Sylvia Plath as a 'confessional poet' breaks down here because these poems work on so many more levels than on the personal alone. 'Winter Trees', dated 29 November 1962, which was to become the title poem of the last volume of her poetry published posthumously, is a good example of the power of this multi-faceted writing.

The poem is very short, consisting of three stanzas of five lines each. The sound patterns create an impression of echoing, through the repetition of -ing (drawing, ring, wedding, chanting, nothing) of *s* and *t* and *v* and *w*. This is a piece that has to be read slowly, forcing the reader to linger over the words in a kind of chant. In the first verse, the trees emerge from the fog and are compared to a blurred drawing. Fog is 'their blotter', the sky is a mass of 'wet dawn inks'. In this unreal time, memories grow and spread 'ring on ring,/a series of weddings'. The compression of imagery in these two lines creates an effect of richness; the word 'ring' has connotations of sound, of marriage, of wholeness, of ancient tree trunks enduring through time and, most obviously here, of the immediate comparison with ink and water seeping into blotting paper in circular patterns.

The second verse personifies the trees. They are 'truer than women', they know 'neither abortions nor bitchery'. They are blessed with the power to recreate themselves – 'they seed so easily' and are in touch with the 'footless', footloose winds and steeped in history.

The constancy of the trees together with their independence and self-sufficiency is admired by the narrator.

In the third verse, another aspect of tree life is introduced. The trees are 'full of wings, other worldliness'. Birds have settled in them, taken them over. The second line of the poem notes ominously that 'in this they are Ledas', a reference to the woman who was raped by Jupiter, disguised as a swan. The reference to God is developed in the next two lines with consciously religious language:

> O mother of leaves and sweetness
> Who are these pietàs?

Leda was the woman violated by the god of classical mythology, Mary the mother of the Christian god, doomed to hold the dead body of her only son. The pain suffered by these women cannot be eased and the last line of the poem returns to the imagery of love and rings of the first verse but quietly states:

> The shadows of ringdoves chanting, but easing nothing.

Sylvia Plath's love poems cover an enormously wide range of experience. There are poems of passion, of exaltation, poems of jealousy and bitterness, poems of savage anger and poems written as though in a stage beyond love. Through these shifts of feeling the poetry and the prose also come to explore some of the contradictions within male–female relationships and many of her ideas prefigure later feminist writers. The only constant love poems are those to and about her children for here there seems to have been a love freed from ambiguity. Men might be faithless, women eavesdrop and deceive with false professions of friendship but, as she writes in 'Kindness', written just days before her death, 'what is so real as the cry of a child?'

6
Poetry and Survival

A confessional poet, an extremist poet, a post-romantic poet, a pre-feminist poet, a suicidal poet – all these terms have been used (and are still being used) in attempts to define and explain Sylvia Plath's writing. Some critics have seen her as schizoid, carrier of a death wish that they perceive in everything she ever wrote. Others have seen her as the victim of male brutality, destroyed by a faithless husband, having been undermined by an ambitious mother, over compensating for her own inadequate marriage. There will no doubt be other equally extravagant 'explanations' of her writing in the future, since, like the works of Keats, with whom she shares the dubious honour of having died young, her writing does not slot easily into categories and headings.

Working on Sylvia Plath's poetry and prose for many years, reading the secondary source material, talking to people who knew her and, by no means least, writing my own poetry, I find it impossible to accept any of these glib definitions, these reductions and over simplifications of a complex personality and multi-faceted writer. Her writing simply does not fit into these easy categories. Some of her poems do indeed appear to be written in the confessional mode but not many of them; some of them might have been written by someone well acquainted with the feminism of the late sixties but some of them decidedly not; some of them show a fascination with death, others equally show delight in life and in living. Nor do the poems show a steady progress towards suicide. Read with hindsight, it can be seen that she went through several stages of anger, despair, grief, quietness and longing for an end to pain but those stages are not part of a steady movement towards dying. In a note in *Encounter*, Ted Hughes wrote:

> It is impossible that anyone could have been more in love with life, or more capable of happiness, than she was.[1]

117

Other friends and acquaintances have expressed similar astonishment that she could have taken her own life. Alvarez asserts his belief that she had never intended to die at all:

> I am convinced by what I know of the facts that this time she did not intend to die. Her suicide attempt ten years before had been in every sense, deadly serious. She had carefully disguised the theft of the sleeping pills, left a misleading note to cover her tracks, and hidden herself in the darkest, most unused corner of a cellar, rearranging behind her the old firelogs she had disturbed, burying herself away like a skeleton in the nethermost family closet. Then she had swallowed a bottle of fifty sleeping pills. She was found late and by accident, and survived only by a miracle. The flow of life in her was too strong even for the violence she had done it. This, anyway, is her description of the act in *The Bell Jar*; there is no reason to believe it false. So she had learned the hard way the odds against successful suicide; she had learned that despair must be counterpoised by an almost obsessional attention to detail and disguise.

By these lights she seemed, in her last attempt, to be taking care not to succeed.[2] Alvarez' distinction between the first suicide attempt and the second, successful one seems important to bear in mind. A failed suicide attempt at 21, when under enormous academic pressures, is not, after all, so unusual and certainly does not indicate a lasting desire to die. When she killed herself in 1963, ten years later, Sylvia Plath had been living under other kinds of enormous, untenable pressures and it seems far more likely that those pressures were the immediate cause of the depression that led her to take her own life, rather than any romantic notion of the inevitability of self-induced death. Those readers who study her work as a series of prefigurations of suicide will find plenty of references to death, many to suicidal death. But it seems to me to be as absurd to read the poems as death wishes as it is to read the poems as evidence of mental illness. That she could have been judged to be mentally ill and unstable is a sign of the failure of many readers – especially male ones – to understand the dilemmas about which she tried to write. The great outpouring of women's writing over the past twenty years has shown more clearly than anything else could that the problems with which Sylvia Plath wrestled are problems that are by no means unique. What was unique was the way in which she gave voice to those contradictions and fragmented aspects of her personality at a time when other women were still keeping silent.

The most straightforward way to reject the writing-as-prelude-to-dying reading is to go back to the poems and prose and look again at them. *The Bell Jar* is a novel about a suicide attempt that fails; but it is also a novel about a woman who learns how to live with herself and how to come to terms with the world, that world of destruction and horror that is described in the first sentences of the book:

> It was a queer, sultry summer, the summer they electrocuted the Rosenbergs, and I didn't know what I was doing in New York. I'm stupid about executions. The idea of being electrocuted makes me sick, and that's all there was to read about in the papers – goggle-eyed headlines staring up at me on every street corner and at the fusty, peanut-smelling mouth of every subway. It had nothing to do with me, but I couldn't help wondering what it would be like, being burned alive all along your nerves.[3]

When she leaves the hospital at the end of the novel, Esther has no answers – 'all I could see were question marks' – but she has looked into herself and seen the problem areas that she had been trying so hard to conceal – her relationships with men, her difficulties with her mother, the split between her sexual and intellectual lives, her obsession with marriage and social status. She has also learned enough to realise that she cannot erase the past, that the images of pain will never leave her because they are part of her history:

> I remembered everything.
>
> I remembered the cadavers and Doreen and the story of the fig-tree and Marco's diamond and the sailor on the Common and Doctor Gordon's wall-eyed nurse and the broken thermometers and the negro with his two kinds of beans and the twenty pounds I gained on insulin and the rook that bulged between sky and sea like a grey skull.
>
> Maybe forgetfulness, like a kind snow, should numb and cover them. But they were part of me. They were my landscape.[4]

Before *The Bell Jar*, she had written another breakdown story, 'Johnny Panic and the Bible of Dreams', completed in December 1958 but not published until ten years later. In his preface to her collected stories, Ted Hughes discusses her fears about putting her life into her writing and suggests that the Johnny Panic story had tapped 'the molten source of her poetry as none of her poems up to then had'. He sees this story as a turning point and suggests that the writing of stories, despite her intensely hard work and desire to succeed with them, was not her strongest point. The reason he gives is interesting:

> If a story is inevitably a fantasy, and if every fantasy leads eventually to the heart of the labyrinth, her problem was that she could not linger among the outer twists and turns and complications, where the world is still solidly itself and comparatively safe, however thrilling. She had an instant special pass to the centre and she had no choice but to use it. She could no more make up an objective ingenious narrative than she could connect up all the letters in her handwriting, where nearly every symbol seems to sit perched over a gulf. This lighting pass through all the walls of the maze was her real genius. Instant confrontation with the most central, unacceptable things.[5]

If 'Johnny Panic' marks a shift in her prose narrative style, it may be, as Hughes suggests, because it tackles the fearsome issues of madness, suicide and an uncaring world. At the end, when the I-speaker becomes a Christ figure ('the crown of wire' on her head, 'the wafer of forgetfulness' on her tongue) she experiences the horror of electric-shock treatment, the closest she can come to sharing the fate of the Rosenbergs. As someone who had undergone such treatment during her breakdown, Sylvia Plath could write about it 'from the centre', from having been there. It is a story full of bitterness and anguish but the final note is not one of despair and resignation, it is one of anger and anger, despite the references in the words to dying, fuels survival and desire for revenge:

> At the moment when I think I am most lost the face of Johnny Panic appears in a nimbus of arc lights on the ceiling overhead. I am shaken like a leaf in the teeth of glory. His beard is lightning. Lightning is in his eye. His Word changes and illumines the universe.

> The air crackles with his blue-tongued lightning-haloed angels. His love is the twenty-story leap, the rope at the throat, the knife at the heart.

> He forgets not his own.

Sylvia Plath writes her breakdown story and suicide attempt in prose; in poetry she writes other themes. A set of poems written in February–March 1961 arise out of her period in hospital, with her miscarriage and appendicitis. Again, though, this is not an exclusively Plathian preoccupation but one which recurs in the poetry of many twentieth-century women writers, from the Russians to the Americans. Hospital poetry seems to belong more to women writers than to men, partly because the experience of childbirth is often in a hospital context but partly also because the doctor–patient relationship is a very powerful one in female mythology. At its most disarming, it is the basis of the saccharine love stories of romantic fiction between doctors and nurses or doctors and patients; at its most terrifying it is the area in which male power over women's bodies can be most clearly demonstrated. The woman in the hands of the male surgeon experiences a double powerlessness, that of the sexual as well as the medical, and it is probably for this reason that hospital or medical poetry should keep recurring in the work of so many women writers.

'Tulips', dated 18 March 1962, is a poem built on the experience of being a patient in hospital where time seems to have another meaning and extremes of feeling are dulled by the daily routine. The poem is made up of nine seven-line stanzas, each one a separate unit, without the device of the run-on line between verses that Plath so often uses. The end-stopped verses reinforce the feeling of the packaging of time into distinct units of the hospital day. But within that packaging, the mind of the I-speaker ranges out beyond the limits imposed on her. The first line contrasts the stillness within with the desire for movement: 'The tulips are excitable, it is winter here'. The I-speaker has given herself up to the doctors, she has handed herself over:

> I am nobody; I have nothing to do with explosions.
> I have given my name and my day-clothes to the nurses
> And my history to the anaesthetist and my body to the surgeons.

This helplessness is described further in the second verse where the I-speaker has virtually been dismembered by the doctors and nurses – 'They have propped my head between the pillow and the sheet-cuff'. In the third verse her body is compared to a pebble and the medical staff are like water running over it. She has lost all feeling and become a stone. What is more she does not need 'baggage' – the literal baggage of her overnight case and the emotional baggage of the photo of her husband and child.

The fourth verse moves onto another dimension. The I-speaker talks about herself as 'a thirty-year-old cargoboat' who has 'let things slip'. As the rest of her life has slipped out of view, the metaphor of drowning is used – 'the water went over my head'. Purified by this absence she is 'a nun now'. In the fifth verse, dazed with the medically induced peacefulness, she describes freedom as a kind of total stasis:

> I didn't want any flowers, I only wanted
> To lie with my hands turned up and be utterly empty.

In this world of whiteness and motionlessness, the tulips are an intrusion, symbols of the life of activity outside – 'the tulips are too red in the first place, they hurt me', 'the vivid tulips eat my oxygen', 'the tulips should be behind bars like dangerous animals'. The redness of the tulips gradually forces the I-speaker to leave her death-in-life state. They breathe at her 'through the gift paper', they turn their faces to her and in the last two verses, as the pace of the language speeds up and the number of images increases, the tulips become a force for life, bearers of noise in verse 8 and warmth in verse 9, bringing the I-speaker back up out of her drowning state into an awareness of life:

> And I am aware of my heart: it opens and closes
> Its bowl of red blooms out of sheer love of me.
> The water I taste is warm and salt, like the sea,
> And comes from a country far away as health.

'Fever 103°' is a very different medical poem. Dated 20 October 1962, it derives from a period of depression and high fever that is docu-mented in the letters home (it was on 21 October that Sylvia Plath wrote angrily to her mother about the person out of Belsen needing to know that others have been there and survived). 'Fever 103°' is a poem about a descent into hell and is full of images of hell. The first line asks the crucial question about eligibility to enter: 'Pure? What does it mean?' and the reader is drawn in, past three-headed Cerberus 'who wheezes at the gate', into the realm of sin, 'the tinder cries' and 'the indelible smell/of a snuffed candle'. The next line after this image, with the keyword 'snuffed', opens with the word 'love' repeated twice, another example of Sylvia Plath's ability to set words alongside each other in such a way that their fields of connotation open out in all kinds of directions. The 'yellow sullen smokes' that 'roll/from me' are presented as signs of the ever-presence of hell and the reader proceeds through a range of images of suffering ever deeper into the depths – Isadora Duncan, strangled with her own scarf in the wheel of a car, after a lifetime of emotional desolation following the deaths of her two children, 'the aged and the meek' choked to death, the image of the dying baby contrasted with the 'ghastly orchid', the leopard turned white and killed in just an hour by radiation poisoning and, finally, the ultimate horrors of both the speaker's inner life and the world: unfaithfulness in marriage and the atomic bomb

> Greasing the bodies of adulterers
> Like Hiroshima ash and eating in.

The tenth verse opens with a direct address to 'darling'. For three days and nights (the time Dante spent in Hell) she has been unable to eat or drink, in great pain – 'your body/hurts me as the world hurts God' and undergoes a series of metaphorical transformations – 'I am a lantern. . . . All by myself I am a huge camellia. . . .'

> The beads of hot metal fly, and I, love, I
> Am a pure acetylene
> Virgin
> Attended by roses

The bitter, jokey tone of the poem shifts in the last few lines to an enigmatic conclusion. The acetylene virgin ascends to heaven, out of the fires of hell, but alone without you or him, or any man. This last sentence is without a main verb; it is a deliberate syntactical shift that stresses linguistically the breaking down of the old self, glibly able to handle words with fluency and flair:

> Not you, nor him
> Not him, nor him
> (My selves dissolving, old whore petticoats) –
> To Paradise.

In a note for her BBC reading of this poem, Sylvia Plath said:

> it is about two kinds of fire – the fires of hell, which merely agonize, and the fires of heaven, which purify. During the poem, the first sort of fire suffers itself into the second.

Out of the hell of fever and pain, the woman rises up to paradise.
She is a survivor. Between these two poems, Sylvia Plath wrote
another kind of hospital poem, *Three Women*, a piece for BBC radio,
broadcast on 19 August 1962. As the use of personae in her poetry
shows, she had a strong sense of the dramatic and *Three Women* is a
verse play for three female voices.[6] The First Voice is that of a
woman who gives birth to a healthy male child:

> Who is he, this blue furious boy,
> Shiny and strange, as if he had hurtled from a star?
> What did my fingers do before they held him?

The Second Voice is that of a woman who suffers a miscarriage and
loses the child:

> It is usual, they say, for such a thing to happen.
> It is usual in my life, and the lives of others.
> I am one in five, something like that. I am not hopeless.
> I am beautiful as a statistic. Here is my lipstick.

The Third Voice is that of a young student who gives birth to a girl
that is given away for adoption immediately:

> The books I carry wedge into my side.
> I had an old wound once, but it is healing.
> I had a dream of an island, red with cries.
> It was a dream, and did not mean a thing.

On the surface, the three women represent three different moments
of the childbearing process – the satisfied first-time mother, the
sorrowful woman who loses her baby, the immature woman who
gives birth and then renounces the child and returns to her previous
life. But what makes *Three Women* rise above the level of cliché is the
constant variation of viewpoint throughout the piece. Each woman
tells her story, giving her point of view, and there is no definitive
ideological narrative voice that locates the women in any moral
hierarchy: the First Voice begins to speak with authority and patience
'I am slow as the world...I am calm. I am calm' but recognises that
this is a calm that presages something very different. 'It is the calm
before something awful'. Then comes the moment of the child's

birth and all the calmness and stoicism vanish in the pain of the happening:

> I am the centre of an atrocity.
> What pains, what sorrows must I be mothering?

In the next verse, she links that pain with the pain of living in the world:

> Can such innocence kill and kill? It milks my life.
> The trees wither in the street. The rain is corrosive.

Childbirth has a political dimension; producing another human being is to expose that child to the horrors that wait for it in the world, to experience for a few moments the primal pain in which all is terror and chaos:

> My eyes are squeezed by this blackness.
> I see nothing.

But after the birth, that feeling of terror changes. The child born is one of many, brother to the rest of mankind:

> I see them showering like stars on to the world –
> On India, Africa, America, these miraculous ones,
> These pure, small images. They smell of milk.
> Their footsoles are untouched. They are walkers of air.

Faced with this absolute purity that she has to defend, the First Voice meditates on her role as protector: 'How long can I be wall, keeping the wind off?' Sooner or later, she fears, the darkness of life and the pain in the world will reach out and engulf him. But her monologue ends on a note of hopefulness; she has painted his nursery, made his small world as beautiful as possible and wishes for him a life of ordinariness:

> I do not will him to be exceptional . . .
> I will him to be common,
> To love me as I love him,
> And to marry what he wants and where he will.

The Third Voice has a very different style and language. From her first speech she uses short, assertive statements, repeating the cry: 'I wasn't ready'. Later, in her final speech, she repeats another sentence, only this time it is a question: 'What is it that I miss?' Between that first cry of unwillingness and unreadiness and that final question, the Third Voice goes through a series of stages that leave her increasingly troubled and ill at ease. The birth is associated with horror – 'It is a place of shrieks' and the cries of the child when born are like 'hooks that catch and grate like cats'. The cries pierce the mother's side 'like arrows' – and when she leaves her in the hospital she has to undo her fingers 'like bandages'. Leaving the child behind, walking out into the world again with 'the clothes of a fat woman I do not know', she is suddenly afraid:

I am so vulnerable suddenly,
I am a wound walking out of hospital.
I am a wound that they are letting go.
I leave my health behind. I leave someone would adhere to me...

Once outside again, back at college, the wound starts to heal and she is left with the memory of something that has been lost, something that troubles her despite her insistence that 'it is so beautiful to have no attachments'. For the Third Voice, the world is outside the hospital; leaving the child, she leaves behind some part of herself in a place that has been unreal to her. This is in direct contrast with the First Voice for whom the hospital becomes the centre of the world and the source of all creation. The Third Voice is doomed to live with another kind of pain, the pain of loss. Both women learn about suffering through the birth of their children; once the actual pain of the birth itself is over, they are left to deal with the pain of living as mothers, one with the daily fears of what will happen to her child in the world as he grows, the other with the pain of having been briefly a mother but having renounced that role in order to grow in other ways. For neither woman does the future look whole and happy and the underlying significance of this emphasis on sorrow and motherhood is that woman's lot is seen to be a hard one. Men do not feature in their lives as sharers or as easers of their pain.

It is in the speeches of the Second Voice that men are mentioned most frequently. The Second Voice loses her child before birth, hence she does not pass through the gates of childbirth that are marked as an exclusively female rite of passage. Having lost her child, she has lost that special experience – 'I see myself as a shadow, neither man nor woman'. In her first speech the Second Voice describes the first tell-tale sign of the miscarriage but goes on immediately in the next line to talk about the world she now cannot leave, the world of men. Significantly, it is a world of work, an office:

When I first saw it, the small red seep, I did not believe it. I watched the men walk about me in the office. They were so flat!

That image of flatness, of two-dimensionality which she sees as typical of men, is an image that recurs throughout her monologue. In the next line of the first speech, she associates that flatness with inadequacy: 'There was something about them like cardboard and now I had caught it'. The Second Voice tells how she leaves the hospital looking as she did when she came in – 'the mirror gives back a woman without deformity/the nurses give back my clothes, and an identity'. She puts on her make-up, 'the red mouth I put on with my identity', and goes out. Her husband, she says, will understand and will love her as if she had lost 'an eye, a leg, a tongue'. But behind this neat appearance there has been a massive change in her reality. 'How shyly she super-imposes her neat self/on the inferno of African oranges, the heel-hung pigs'. She has experienced a kind of suffering that marks her within. At home, with her husband, quietly mending a silk slip she reflects that 'I think I have been healing'. She holds the pain inside, waiting.

The Second Voice concludes the piece, with the image of herself and her husband sitting quietly together in silence, she with her outward calm and control and inner turmoil, he oblivious, turning the pages of a book. The husband is seen as distant and although she talks about his love and understanding, she also says that he cannot share in what she is feeling. 'I am a wife', she says almost at the end of her monologue and the placing of that four-word statement stresses its ambiguity. What does it mean to be a wife, she seems to be asking, if she is denied a child. The next words return to her pain – 'The city waits and aches'. In the previous verse, the subject of the verbs *ache* and *wait* had been *I*. Now it is the city, the whole world, reality itself that shares her pain with her. Reality, that is, as a woman experiences it not as a man does.

The verse play ends with an image of hope: 'The little grasses/ crack through stone, and they are green with life'. It is an image of beginning, of promise; the city of stone comes alive again and the woman too, in time, will heal and perhaps will succeed in giving

birth. The little grasses of the last lines recall the image of the opening
speech by the First Voice, when she describes herself as attended by
'leaves and petals'. The woman denied the fulfilment of childbirth
waits and hopes for some future moment of fruition.

Unquestionably this is a work that glorifies motherhood as
a uniquely female experience. The woman who renounces her child
cannot, nevertheless, renounce the experience she has undergone,
which has marked her forever in a very special way, just as the
woman who loses the child mourns the loss of participating in that
specialness. But the First Voice, the one who gives birth to a wanted
child, is not held up to the others as an ideal. Her happiness is tem-
pered by anxiety and the source of that worry is living in the world
that creeps in through all kinds of channels. Throughout the poem
there are references to the vastness of the world, in comparison to the
boundaries within which the women move; Africa reaches out even
through the fruit in the shop windows, the shadow of war and the
nuclear bomb, of the thalidomide children, touches the new mother
and her child. The Second Voice makes the gap between the world of
women and the world of men explicit throughout her monologue:

And then there were other faces. The faces of nations,
Governments, parliaments, societies,
The faceless faces of important men.

It is these men I mind:
They are so jealous of anything that is not flat! They are jealous gods
That would have the whole world flat because they are.

Eileen Aird says of Sylvia Plath that her originality

> lies in her insistence that what has been traditionally regarded as
> a woman's world of domesticity, childbearing, marriage, is also
> a world which contains the tragic. She draws from this female world
> themes which are visionary and supernatural; although it is a world
> which is eventually destroyed by death, her work is far from depress-
> ing because of the artistry with which she delineates her vision.[7]

This assessment is a very fair one. Again and again the bleakness of
the content material of one of Sylvia Plath's poems is offset by the
structure and the language which foregrounds the motif of survival.
Three Women ends with the word 'life' and she arranged the poems for

her *Ariel* collection in a deliberate sequence that began with the word 'Love' in 'Morning Song' ('Love set you going like a fat gold watch') and ended with the word 'spring' in 'Wintering' ('The bees are flying. They taste the spring'). Far from foregrounding death there is a conscious effort to foreground life, even when the poems speak of the greatest pain, and it is this characteristic of her poetry which marks Sylvia Plath as a survivor poet, a writer with a message of hope.

Shortly after *Three Women*, Sylvia Plath wrote *Crossing the Water*, a twelve-line poem divided into four stanzas of three lines each, which is, as the title indicates, a poem about transition. There is no I-speaker, instead there are references to us and the final verse is addressed to a *you* that may be an individual or may be the collective reader. The image of flatness, developed in *Three Women*, is strongly present here and the word 'black' or 'blackness' is repeated several times. The opening lines establish the tone of the poem:

> Black lake, black boat, two black, cut-paper people.
> Where do the black trees go that drink here?

The trees, humanised in this way, seem more alive than the people who are reduced to silhouettes, two-dimensional figures of blackness. In the second verse there is a shift of perspective; from the wide-angle image of the lake and the vastness of trees stretching out to 'cover Canada' down to the people in the boat looking at the water lilies whose leaves 'do not wish us to hurry'. But these leaves too are flat and they are also 'full of dark advice'. The people in the boat, like the flowers, trees, even the fishes in the lake are filled with darkness – 'the spirit of blackness is in us'.

The ninth line of the poem introduces a whole new set of images: a snag in the water 'is lifting a valedictory, pale hand'. This is an image from Arthurian romance recalling the passing of Arthur, the moment when the white hand emerged from the dark lake to take back Arthur's sword, symbol of the now-lost unity of the Round Table. As in 'Lyonnesse', there is a deliberate reference to the end of idealism through the image of the end of Arthur's dream of an ideal society. The last verse of the poem goes beyond the lake, beyond the immediacy of the blackness, into a quasi-dreamlike state:

> Stars open among the lilies.
> Are you not blinded by such expressionless sirens?
> This is the silence of astounded souls.

Who is the you-figure, blinded by the silence of the lilies? Floating on the water's surface, the lilies seem to be inviting the people in the boat to join them and sink down beneath the black water. In Arthurian legend, the arm rising from the lake is evidence of the supernatural, of the fairy kingdom that finally takes Arthur back to live forever waiting for the moment to return. In this poem, the dark water remains an enigma; the stars among the lilies may be beckoning to death or to a state beyond death, a mystical point of stasis where no pain exists and all is silence.

Despite stylistic differences, there are close links with 'Winter Landscape with Rooks' from 1956. There is the same dark water, the same use of contrast with a flash of white (a swan in the first poem, lilies in the second), the same use of landscape to create a physical image of a state of mind. The close links between the imagery of these two poems is further evidence of the validity of Ted Hughes' analysis of her work as a unified whole, through which patterns of imagery, themes and symbols recur consistently. In the last year of her life, Sylvia Plath wrote several poems that have been described as mystical though whether this is evidence of a religious conversion, as some critics have suggested, is a debatable point. What seems most likely is that emotional crises through which she was passing caused her to reconsider various strands of her own existence. Earlier, in December 1958, she had noted in her Journal that

> Writing is a religious act: it is an ordering, a reforming, a relearning and reloving of people and the world as they are and as they might be. A shaping which does not pass away like a day of typing or a day of teaching. The writing lasts: it goes about on its own in the world.

'Years' and 'Mary's Song', for example, both written in November 1962, are poems with a strong sense of mysticism as is an appropriately titled poem dated 1 February 1963, 'Mystic'. As with many of the poems from the last year, questions are asked and answers are not given. In 'Mystic', the question that is repeated over and over is 'what is the remedy?' Once one has seen God, the I-speaker asks, what is the remedy? How can the experience be put out of mind when memory brings it back continuously? The god, however, does not seem to be the Christian God, despite the many overtly Christian references to cathedrals, the communion tablet, even to Christ himself. Rather God is symbolic of something or someone that the I-speaker has encountered and loved and cannot forget. 'Meaning leaks from molecules', 'the air is a mill of hooks', the speaker of the poem cannot escape from the memories of the vision of perfection that she once believed was possible. Yet even here, despite the sadness, the poem ends on a hopeful note:

> The chimneys of the city breathe, the window sweats,
> The children leap in their cots.
> The sun blooms, it is a geranium.
> The heart has not stopped.

The suffering heart can still experience the daily life of a city, still reach out towards the energy of children and the colour of flowers. Whatever remedy is sought, the poem seems to answer itself. The remedy is living, it is continuing to experience those parts of life that are beautiful, despite the encounter in the past with God.

Besides the mystical poems, the poems in which the struggle for happiness competes with the forces that bring despair and hopelessness, there are also poems that show a strong awareness of the historical moment through which Sylvia Plath was passing. Just as she seems to have thought deeply about the significance of religious experience once the greatest pain was over, so she also seems to use images from the world to describe her own inner feelings. In an interview with Peter Orr she describes her new interest in studying history:

> I am very interested in Napoleon. at the present: I'm very interested in battles, in wars, in Gallipoli, the First World War and so on, and I think that as I age I am becoming more and more historical. I certainly wasn't at all in my early twenties.[8]

Napoleon, 'The hump of Elba on your short back', provides one of the central images for 'The Swarm', one of the five bee poems written in October 1962. He fuses with the beekeeper, the 'man with gray hands', who comes to the village to catch and hive the swarm which is taken from the freedom of the high trees to its 'new mausoleum'. Susan Van Dyne has studied the bee poems in manuscript form, looking at the changes in the drafts, and she suggests a reading for 'The Swarm' that integrates the motif of the retreat from Moscow and Napoleon's plundering of Europe, the details of the capture of the bees and the reference in the third line of the poem to jealousy – 'Jealousy can open the blood'. In Van Dyne's reading, Sylvia Plath is linking her Napoleon with Ted Hughes, the 'little man', as she described him after the break-up, and there is a level of autobiographical statement running through the poem which utilises the historical references metaphorically. History, and everyday experiences became equally material sources for poetic expression. Susan Van Dyne states her view that the entire bee sequence of poems represents 'Plath's struggle to bring forth an articulate, intelligible self from the death-box of the hive'.[9] Her essay is very useful in shedding light on the way in which Sylvia Plath created her poems, carefully selecting words and phrases, listing her own alternatives. She shows, for example, the way in which the final, assertive line of 'Wintering' went through a series of stages of doubt, when the poet seemed unable to move beyond questioning. As it stands, that final verse reads as follows:

Will the hive survive, will the gladiolas
Succeed in banking their fires
To enter another year?
What will they taste of, the Christmas roses? The bees are flying.
They taste the spring.

The questions remain unanswered in that last line but the sureness of these two short sentences gives the reader an impression of hope. That hope was certainly not so clear in the versions listed by Van Dyne:

> Snow water? Corpses? (Thin, sweet Spring.)
> (A sweet Spring?) Spring?
> (Impossible spring?)
> (What sort of spring?)
> (O God, let them taste of spring.)

The form of the question, the use of adjectives to qualify the noun 'spring', the wish form of the last alternative are all syntactically weaker than the final version with its short, tight statements. The bee poems bring together a complex web of narrative threads, from Sylvia Plath's autobiography and her other writing, but the clearest single line through them all is the exploration of the meaning of power and freedom. In the first of the sequence, 'The Bee Meeting', the I-speaker is met by a group of villagers who dress her in a bee-keeper's veil. She appears to be their victim, unable to escape from the task they have imposed on her – 'I could not run without having to run for ever' – and as the villagers hunt the old queen bee, so the I-speaker and the queen fuse together and the last verse of the poem might equally be spoken by either woman or bee.

In the second poem, 'The Arrival of the Bee Box', the I-speaker listens to the buzzing of the furious bees within the box and wonders what would happen if she were to let them loose. By the last lines of the poem she has decided. The bees will not attack her since she is 'no source of honey' so she will take on herself the power to release them:

> Tomorrow I will be sweet God, I will set them free.
> The box is only temporary.

In 'Stings', the third poem, the I-speaker states explicitly 'I am in control'. She and the old queen bee share past imprisonment; the one is old, 'her wings torn shawls, her long body/robbed of its plush', and the other has suffered from servitude: 'for years I have eaten dust/and dried plates with my dense hair'. Both woman and queen bee 'stand in a column/of winged, unmiraculous women'. But in the last verse of the poem, the queen comes out to claim her own like an avenging angel:

> Now she is flying
> More terrible than she ever was, red
> Scar in the sky, red comet
> Over the engine that killed her –
> The mausoleum, the wax house.

The battle continues in 'The Swarm' when the bees are captured and taken prisoner by the man with grey hands. For a time, it seems, the male power of the beekeeper has triumphed. But in the last poem, 'Wintering', that triumph is turned around, as female bees and the woman become the survivors of the winter cold and the bringers of new life:

> The bees are all women,
> Maids and the long royal lady.
> They have got rid of the men,

The blunt clumsy stumblers, the boors.
Winter is for women –
The woman still at her knitting,
At the cradle of Spanish walnut,
Her body a bulb in the cold and too dumb to think.

'This is the time of hanging on for the bees' says the I-speaker in the fifth verse of the poem and equally it is a time of hanging on for the woman with her child and her knitting. Once through the winter they will share in the coming of spring and new life. It is ironic that, despite this promise, Sylvia Plath was not to see the next spring after all.

The battles of which she spoke in her interview rage through many of the poems in the autumn–winter of 1962–63. 'The disks of the brain revolve, like the muzzles of canon' she says in 'The Courage of Shutting-Up'; in 'Daddy', the Polish town is 'scraped flat by the roller/of wars, wars, wars'; the sleeping capsule in 'The Jailer' is a 'red and blue zeppelin' that drops the speaker 'from a terrible altitude'. Most potent of all, the image of the concentration camps and the destruction of the Jews runs through many poems, such as 'Daddy', 'Lady Lazarus' and 'Getting There'. This image is linked to another central twentieth-century image of total devastation, that of the nuclear holocaust. In 'Mary's Song', dated 19 November 1962, these images combine with other motifs – the fears of the mother for her child, the necessity of sacrifice, regeneration after suffering.

'Mary's Song' is a poem made up of seven three-line stanzas, linked by the imagery which proceeds through a series of thought-leaps. The opening line presents an image from everyday life: 'The Sunday lamb cracks in its fat' but then immediately that sentence acquires symbolic overtones in the next two lines: 'the fat/sacrifices its opacity...'. The lamb that is being cooked is equated to the lamb that was Mary's child, the Christ child. The image of the fat losing its texture and thickness and becoming translucent is taken up in the second verse, where the golden colour of the fat is a 'holy gold'. The fire that melts the fat, making it edible ('precious') also burns people – heretics and Jews – and the fourth verse stresses the permanence of those historical persecutions as symbols of man's inhumanity:

> Their thick palls float
> Over the cicatrix of Poland, burnt-out
> Germany.
> They do not die.

The past with all its horrors remains part of the present, the images of death cannot be set aside. In the fifth verse the I-speaker appears for the first time with an image of suffering – 'gray birds obsess my heart'. The grey birds that bear the message of death from the past move us on to the possibility of future destruction in the next line – 'Mouth-ash, ash of eye' – where the word 'ash' carries connotations of nuclear death. The ashes of burned bodies, the glowing ovens become the whole universe in the sixth verse and in the seventh that universe turns into a psychic landscape:

> It is a heart,
> This holocaust I walk in,
> O golden child the world will kill and eat.

'Mary's Song' recalls the fears of the First Voice in *Three Women*, uncertain how long she will be able to protect her child from the world's evils. Mary's case should be different, since the death of her child is a symbol of human regeneration, but the emphasis in this poem is on the power of history and the horrors of the past to reach out and touch the present. Mary must accept the inevitability of suffering.

Anne Cluysenaar discusses Sylvia Plath in terms of someone who is a 'survivor' in the clinical sense of the term. She describes her as 'a typical "survivor" in the psychiatric sense', arguing that 'as an element in this complex of emotions, imagining death has a life-enhancing function'. The fictionalising of death becomes an assertion of power over death. Anne Cluysenaar sees the central message of her writing as being:

> The retention of discrimination and the will to speak, the will to communicate. Her determination not to accept relief from any ready-made dogma is admirable.[10]

The poems are a testament to struggle and the *Ariel* poems particularly show a determination to survive that overrides all the imagery of death and horror. In the event, *Ariel* was never published in the order that she had wanted it and the collection was ultimately over-shadowed by *Winter Trees*, which contained the last poems she ever wrote, together with *Three Women*. The disparity between her structure for *Ariel* and the volume that finally appeared is most obvious in the different emphasis on hope and survival. Her structure would have

led the reader towards faith in the continuation of the struggle. As
we have received the poems since her death, the emphasis has
shifted onto a reading of the poems which perceives them as prefigurations of her end. She has become a writer who wrote her own
epitaph during her lifetime.

Margaret Uroff sums up the achievement of *Ariel* in fitting terms:

> *Ariel* must be read as several chapters of a creative autobiography,
> written by a woman whose purpose in the last years of her life
> was to come to terms with the various female roles and identities
> into which she had been split. It is full of wrong leads, frustrated
> efforts, obscure and private battles that attest to the difficulties she
> had to face and to the energy she expended on them. Her final
> poetic accomplishment was not to transcend these hardships, but
> to face them directly and to leave a record of that confrontation. In
> the image of the rising lioness/Virgin/red comet, she identified
> a female figure violent enough to triumph in a world that Plath
> imagined would reduce the woman to a jade statue – but a female
> also with creatively violent powers of her own.[11]

The poems read as epitaphs belong to the last days in February 1963.
On 1 February she wrote 'Mystic', 'Kindness' and 'Words'. Three
days later, on 4 February, came 'Contusion' and on 5 February the
two last poems, 'Balloons' and 'Edge'. Two of these, 'Contusion' and
'Edge', are poems in which any semblance of struggle has been
abandoned; they are perhaps the saddest of all her works. The four
sparse verses of 'Contusion' offer, through the means of a distant
third-person narrator, a vision of stasis and silence. The first two
lines contrast the dull purple of the bruise with the whiteness of the
deathly body:

> Colour floods to the spot, dull purple.
> The rest of the body is all washed out

The pearly whiteness of the body of the third line carries connotations
of death; years before, Plath had described her father as Neptune
with his conch shell ('On the Decline of Oracles'), which in turn was
an image derived from T. S. Eliot and Shakespeare's *The Tempest*
('Full fathom five thy father lies'). Whose death, whose body are
never defined in this poem but the very absence of clarification
emphasises the sense of despair. The third-person narrator makes

statements in a cold, detached manner that belies the content material. The last three lines are three simple sentences, each containing an image of ending:

> The heart shuts,
> The sea slides back,
> The mirrors are sheeted.

'Edge' continues from that image of the covered mirror. Narrated in the third person it describes someone only as 'the woman', whose dead body 'wears the smile of accomplishment'. Robed in a Greek toga, her dead children 'coiled' beside her, 'folded...back into her body as petals/of a rose close', she is observed from a distance. The last two verses introduce the image of the greatest watcher of all, the moon:

> She is used to this sort of thing.
> Her blacks crackle and drag.

The dead woman is a kind of statue, a monument to herself, watched by the old moon in her hag phase. The woman and her children 'have come so far, it is over' and the poem seems to suggest that this decision of ending should be accepted for what it is – a statement of finality. The moon, ancient goddess and muse, need not grieve, for this is neither unexpected nor unusual. She has seen it many times before when a woman gives up the struggle to juggle the many facets of her life. And yet the woman who wrote 'Edge' also wrote the beautiful 'Balloons' on the same day, in which she compares the 'globes of thin air, red, green' to 'wishes or free/ peacocks blessing/old ground with a feather'. Two such different poems, one rejoicing in the mobility of life and the other praising the dignity and silence of death.

Reading Sylvia Plath's Journal, the swings of mood show up very clearly. She records moments of ecstasy, enthusiasm, anger, pain and black depression. An entry for 13 October 1959 details one such depression:

> Very depressed today. Unable to write a thing. Menacing gods. I feel outcast on a cold star, unable to feel anything but an awful helpless numbness. I look down into the warm, earthy world. Into a nest of lovers' beds, baby cribs, meal tables, all the solid

commerce of life in this earth, and feel apart, enclosed in a wall of glass.

Perhaps, on that morning of 11 February 1963, the glass walls descended round her once again and she was too exhausted to fight back. The last lines of 'Ariel' say all that needs to be said:

> And now I
> Foam to wheat, a glitter of seas.
> The child's cry
>
> Melts in the wall.
> And I
> Am the arrow,
>
> The dew that flies
> Suicidal, at one with the drive
> Into the red
>
> Eye, the cauldron of morning.

7

Plath Translated: Ted Hughes' *Birthday Letters*

The publication of Ted Hughes' *Birthday Letters* in 1998 was perceived generally as an extraordinary literary event, for Hughes had consistently sought to maintain silence and not to engage in public debates about his relationship with Sylvia Plath. He completed the manuscript a year earlier, and in January 1998 a selection of the poems with a commentary by Erica Wagner was published in *The Times*. In her biography of Hughes, Elaine Feinstein notes that as early as 1989 he had apparently told Carolyne Wright, a young translator in Bangladesh that he was writing poems about his private life,[1] but when the poems appeared the literary world was astounded. The collection won the Forward Prize for Poetry and entered the British best-selling books lists. Hughes' decision to break his long-standing silence had a huge impact, and through the poems we are able to look again not only at their relationship as husband and wife, but also at the relationship between two great writers, one of whom poured out all the violence that was in her heart while the other refused almost to speak her name for decades.

This chapter will look at *Birthday Letters*, not only as an instrument that furthers understanding of the life and work of Sylvia Plath, but also as a kind of translation of Plath's own writing. Hughes was always interested in translation, and his other best-selling collection had appeared a year before *Birthday Letters*. *Tales from Ovid* is a rendering of passages from the Latin poet Ovid, reshaped for the contemporary reader, and in a similar way, *Birthday Letters* reshapes the life and the Journals, letters and poems Sylvia Plath left behind. Hughes had been interested in promoting translation since the 1960s, when he founded the Journal, *Modern Poetry in Translation* together with Daniel Weissbort, and in his latter years his translation output increased. *Birthday Letters* is therefore both an original collection of startlingly personal works, and a translation of the work of another poet, a translation that, as all good translations must, reconstructs and re-examines the texts that provide the point of departure.

Different strands run through the collection of 88 poems of varying length, written at different times across a twenty-five year span. One poem, 'Freedom of Speech' refers to Plath's sixtieth birthday, which would have been 27 October 1992, while 'The Visit' refers to an experience ten years after her death. The poems are arranged in a rough (but by no means consistent) chronological order, and move around in time, now retelling an event that Plath also relates in her writings, now remembering, now moving into the realm of the symbolic and the imaginary.

'The Visit', the fourth poem in the collection, recounts a struggle between memories that are still sharply felt with another version of the same event that alters those memories. The poem begins with an account of the incident when Lucas Myers and Hughes, both drunk, threw stones at what they thought was Plath's bedroom window, only to learn afterwards that it was the wrong window. Then the mood changes, and the line 'aiming to find you, and missing, and again missing' assumes another layer of meaning, beyond the simple act of stone-throwing:

> Flinging earth at a glass that could not protect you
> because you were not there

The 'earth' that is thrown is a reminder of the grave, the glass an echo of the bell jar within which Plath saw herself as imprisoned. Then the poem shifts gear, moving directly to Plath's own writing and to Hughes' feelings as he read her version of the same incident in her Journal. Her entry for 10 March 1956 reads:

HE is here; in Cambridge. Smiling blub-faced Bert, all scrubbed and polished, met me in the street on the way to the College library: 'Lucas and Ted threw stones at your window last night.' A huge joy galloped through me; they remembered my name, it was the wrong window and I was out drinking with Hamish, but they exist in this world (p. 232).

Hughes describes his own mixed feelings when he first read her words:

> Ten years after your death
> I meet on a page of your journal, as never before,

> The shock of your joy
> When you heard of that
>
> . . . .
>
> Suddenly I read all this –
> Your actual words, as they floated
> Out through your throat and tongue and onto your page –

This moment of recognition instantly dissolves into another memory, from 'years ago now', of Hughes' little daughter asking 'Daddy, where's Mummy?', which in turn triggers a memory of digging at frozen soil just after Plath's death, the numbness of the earth reflecting his own icy grief. The last lines of the poem move from that moment of encounter between the poet and his dead wife through memory and writing to a deeply sad acknowledgement of the limitations of words:

> I look up – as if to meet your voice
> With all its urgent future
> That has burst in on me. Then look back
> At the book of the printed words.
> You are ten years dead. It is only a story.
> Your story. My story.

In his memoir of Hughes and Plath, Lucas Myers writes about his own reading of 'The Visit' and notes tellingly:

> It is always surprising, if you know of events first hand, to see how utterly historians and biographers get things wrong even when they are trying to get them right. When they are trying to get them to fit a thesis (i.e. trying to get them wrong), it is not at all surprising, as can be seen in publications ranging from Chinese versions of the history of Tibet to most of what has been written about Ted and Sylvia.[2]

Myers relates how he wrote to Hughes expressing doubts about *Birthday Letters* because of the intensely personal nature of the material. He was concerned because he distrusted what he called 'first person' poems and felt that this mode of writing was unlike the Hughes whose work he knew and admired. Hughes replied with an account of how he had first come to write poems about his experience of Plath. 'Every circumstance made it so taboo and unmentionable, had actually blocked my whole inner life' Hughes wrote. Myers acknowledges that for Hughes, writing these poems was a catharsis, and points out that Hughes believed poetry was similar to shamanic practice and in consequence could summon up healing energy. He also adds that had Hughes simply wanted to present an alternative version of events, he would have written different poems. This is certainly true, and he would also have ordered the poems very differently.

In an interview with Eilat Negev in 1996 Hughes amplified the reasons given to Lucas Myers in his letter. He pointed out that the shock of Plath's death and the need to care for their two small children drove him to stay silent about Plath for a long time. With the suicide of Assia Weevill in 1969, the woman for whom he had left Plath, who gassed herself with their little girl, Hughes' pain was redoubled. Then, as he tells Eilat Negev, he began to think he should write about the experiences that had been so central to his younger life:

> so I wrote a few poems, including *You Hated Spain*, about our life together. And the effect it had on me was so great, I was sorry I hadn't done it before. Writing released a bizarre dream life, and I realised how much had been locked up inside me.[3]

'You Hated Spain' is one of several poems about the couple's honeymoon in Europe. The poem depicts the deep divisions between Plath and Hughes in terms of their backgrounds and taste, divisions at that time unrecognised and unacknowledged but which were to run like fault lines through the marriage. 'Spain frightened you,' the poem begins, 'Spain/Where I felt at home.' The poet notes how nothing in Plath's previous life had equipped her for this strange country, land of 'the wrought-iron grille, death and the Arab drum'. Spain and its traditions are absent from Plath's world, and become frightening to her, a 'bobby-sox American', yearning for the familiarity of 'college America'. In this poem, Hughes traces what was to become a major theme through *Birthday Letters* – the cultural abyss between the Yorkshire man and the Boston woman.

Critics have not laid much emphasis on Plath's Americanness, nor is it very evident in her poems. Occasionally there are hints of her uneasiness with England and its unfamiliar rituals and patterns of behaviour, and her letters and Journals reveal this more clearly, but the gap between Plath's American world and Hughes' world as depicted in *Birthday Letters* is very wide indeed. Another poem about the honeymoon is entitled 'Your Paris', and in it Hughes contrasts the Paris that Plath experienced with his own. Hers is a city constructed from images of Impressionist paintings and the work of American writers like Ernest Hemingway, Scott Fitzgerald, Henry Miller and Gertrude Stein, it is a literary and artistic city, though also, as the poem reminds us, a city full of painful memories for her, since her relationship with Richard Sassoon had ended in Paris not long before she met Hughes.

Paris for Hughes, in contrast, is not a city of passion or of art, it is a city that reminds him of the horrors of the Second World War:

> I kept my Paris from you. My Paris
> Was only just not German. The capital
> Of the Occupation and old nightmare
> . . . .
> My Paris was a post-war utility survivor,
> The stink of fear still hanging in the wardrobes,
> *Collaborateurs* barely out of their twenties

Plath and Hughes, this poem suggests, had totally different histories, as well as totally different personalities. As they walk round the city, 'my fingers linked in yours', they experience the cultural difference that language cannot bridge. Hughes ironically depicts his inability to understand his wife in terms of inadequate translation. As he tries to understand what he refers to as her 'gushy burblings'

> which I decoded
> Into a language, utterly new to me
> With conjectural, hopelessly wrong meanings

he is left bewildered, unable to interpret the signs even though he tries. This, too is another thread that runs through *Birthday Letters*, the doomed attempts to communicate, doomed because each was using a different language despite the fact that superficially it may have seemed like the same one.

Some of the poems touch on the difference between Plath as city woman and Hughes as countryman. 'The Owl', located in the book just before 'Your Paris', describes how the poet came to see his familiar English world anew through his wife – 'through your eyes it was foreign'. Hawthorn bushes, common mallards, Hughes' ability to make realistic animal sounds in the dark are all received 'with incredulous joy'. In this act of interpretation, whereby he tries to show her his world and at the same time comes to see it differently there is great joy and, for the space of the poem, union between them. But here too the poet hints at communication problems. Plath is 'a camera/recording reflections you could not fathom'. In her poem 'Owl', written in 1958, the bird is 'pale, raptorial', a creature in control of the currents, whereas Hughes' owl is deceived by the man who can so ably imitate the sound of a rabbit and swoops out of the darkness, 'taking me for a post'.

'The Rabbit Catcher', a poem in the latter part of *Birthday Letters* shows none of the joy of the early poem. The scenario is one of a domestic row. The babies have been 'hurled into the car', Plath is driving in a state of 'dybbuk fury' through Cornish country lanes. The conflict is laid out in terms of their habitual culture clash: 'You/ Raged against our English private greed', 'You despised England's grubby edges when you got there', only now as the enemy, she is not described as American but as German ('Your Germanic scowl'), a reference to her ancestry and a motif that becomes ever more pre-valent through *Birthday Letters*. In this state of mutual antagonism they walk along the cliff-top, where Plath sees a line of snares and tears them up, one after another, weeping with rage. Hughes describes his own feelings – 'I was aghast' – at the desecration of ancient country practice, and subtly portrays their completely different world-pictures in a few lines:

> I saw
> Country poverty raising a penny,
> Filling a Sunday stewpot. You saw baby-eyed
> Strangled innocents, I saw sacred
> Ancient custom.

Hughes sees the rabbit catching in terms of ancient rural practice, part of his heritage. He stresses the political implications of the countryman's right to trap for food – 'hard-won concessions/From the hangings and the transportations/To live off the land.' But he also shows how Plath can see none of this: she sees the rabbit catchers as murderers – 'You saw blunt fingers, blood in the cuticles,/Clamped round a blue mug.' The reference here is to the fifth verse of Plath's poem from May 1962 also entitled 'The Rabbit Catcher' where she writes 'I felt hands round a tea mug, dull, blunt,/Ringing the white china.' She imagines the rabbit catcher waiting excitedly to go out and collect his prey, the dead rabbits in the snare 'like sweethearts', exciting him in anticipation.

Plath's poem sketches an evil place, 'the wind gagging my voice...the malignity of gorse' where she discovers the snares, 'set close, like birth pangs'. The poem moves from the malignant landscape to the horror of the silent snares, the man waiting at home with his mug of tea and then in the final verse to an identification with the creatures that are doomed to be destroyed, though here the identification is set out in terms of a failed marriage:

> And we, too, had a relationship –
> Tight wires between us,
> Pegs too deep to uproot, and a mind like a ring
> Sliding shut on some quick thing,
> The constriction killing me also.

Years after reading that poem, writing his own version, Hughes sadly notes that 'in those snares/You'd caught something', something he failed to understand. The last lines of his poem close with another image of hands, hands that forge poetry in some arcane sacrificial ritual that lies outside his comprehension:

> Those terrible, hypersensitive
> Fingers of your verse closed round it and
> Felt it alive. The poems, like smoking entrails,
> Came soft into your hands.

The end of the marriage is portrayed in a poem that comes roughly half way through the volume, 'Epiphany', where the clash between rural and urban as two different mental states is rendered through the story of the poet's encounter one evening with a boy on Chalk Farm Bridge. The boy has a fox cub in his jacket and offers it to the poet for a pound.

The poet hesitates, asking himself how a fox could ever be compatible with the domestic life he is now living. He watches the fox, sees it as lost and in need, but cannot focus his thoughts on how best to respond:

> My thoughts felt like big, ignorant hounds
> Circling and sniffing around him.

He leaves the fox and walks on, 'and dived as if escaping/Into the Underground'. The poem ends with a string of sentences starting with 'if' and four powerful lines that resonate with pain:

> If I had grasped that whatever comes with a fox
> Is what tests a marriage and proves it a marriage –
> I would not have failed the test. Would you have failed it?
> But I failed. Our marriage had failed.

The fox is central to Hughes' conceptualisation of the poet's world. One of his best-known poems is 'The Thought-Fox', that he published in 1957 in his first collection, *The Hawk in the Rain* which was dedicated simply 'To Sylvia'. In this poem, the poet imagines a fox padding softly through the forest as he sits in his room trying to write. The creative animal energy that is the fox is equated with poetic inspiration. In the first verse, the poet sits listening to the ticking clock aware that somewhere, 'something else is alive'. In the last verse, that other life has become fused with his – 'with a sudden sharp hot stink of fox/it enters the dark hole of the head'. Writing about this poem, in *Poetry in the Making*, Hughes says that every time he reads his poem, the fox comes out of the darkness again and steps into his head:

> So, you see, in some ways my fox is better than an ordinary fox.
> It will live forever, it will never suffer from hunger or hounds.
> I have it with me wherever I go. And I made it. And all through
> imagining it clearly and finding the living words.[4]

What Hughes has failed to do, as he suggests in 'Epiphany' is find the right words with which to communicate with his wife. This is, in fact, the epiphany of the title – he realises as he abandons the fox cub to its fate that he has failed, and the failure is not that he cannot save the fox, but that he cannot communicate with the woman he loves. Just as the fox in 'The Thought-Fox' provides him with an image of poetic inspiration, so here the fox cub offers him a sign of failure.

The twin themes of cultural difference and miscommunication recur time and again in *Birthday Letters*. Even in the joyous times, depicted in some of the early poems in the collection, there are hints of what is to come. 'Fate Playing' is a poem about mistiming. She has gone to meet him at Victoria bus station, he has taken a train to King's Cross. She panics and despairs, then manages to cross London where she finds him. The lovers are united, but through the poem are scattered references to her foreignness, her Americanness – 'I was lost and at large/Somewhere in England'...'Because your London was still a kaleidoscope/Of names and places any jolt could scramble'...'Your jolly taxi-driver, laughing, like a small god,/To see an American girl being so American.' Also running through the poem are references to another cultural difference, one that grows in significance through the volume: Plath is increasingly depicted in language and images that recall classical myth. Here she is a wild bacchante figure, with 'molten face...molten eyes' praying to her own gods, driving her chariot to victory, engulfing her lover in her final triumph. In later poems she becomes a gladiator, a religious fanatic, sometimes sacrificial victor, sometimes the slayer.

The autobiographical story traced through the first poems in the volume highlight events, people and most especially, places. 'St Botolph's' centres on the party where Hughes and Plath met, the night when she bit his cheek and left marks in his face. She records this in her entry for 26 February 1956. '18 Rugby Street' recounts the inevitability of the forces that pulled the lovers together. In this poem, which begins with ominous hints of darkness and foreboding, the house is a labyrinth, it is possessed, the tragic deaths of some of the other inhabitants are foretold. It ends with three lines that are a direct reference to John Donne's 'Elegy: To His Mistress Going to Bed'. Hughes, like Donne, is discovering a new continent:

> You were a new world. My new world.
> So this is America, I marvelled.
> Beautiful, beautiful America!

'55 Eltisley' is a much darker poem. The first line 'Our first home has forgotten us' sets the tone. Hughes recalls their moving into the house, where the blood of the previous inhabitant's husband was a dark stain on a pillow. That stain is an ominous symbol for the future, like the blood staining the carpet in the house of Atreus. Here again, though, the poet insists on the cultural divide. The bloodstain confirms:

> Your idea of England: part
> Nursing home, part morgue
> For something partly dying, partly dead.

In the grubby house, Hughes studies the bloodstain and wonders about the history of the house, Plath scrubs the kitchen in 'a fury of scouring'. Later, through their first winter, he declares he was 'happy to stare at a candle', but notes her aversion to cold and her longing for a perfect American world.

A number of poems in *Birthday Letters* are set in America. The first of these, 'The Chipmunk' is another of Hughes' animal poems and records his joy at seeing a chipmunk for the first time in a land where Plath is 'Alien to me as a window-model,/American, airport-hopping super product'. This poem is placed right after 'Wuthering Heights', a 'translation' of a poem by Plath, with the same title, written in September 1961. Hughes describes Plath as 'twice as ambitious as Emily', a reference to Emily Bronte, who was perhaps the most driven by ambition of all three Bronte sisters. This theme, of Plath's desire for fame, her burning ambition to succeed as a writer is increasingly present in the poems that follow.

Both poems centre around a walk across the moors near Haworth. In 1961, Plath wrote several landscape poems, including 'Stars over the Dordogne', 'Blackberrying' and 'Finisterre'. Margaret Dickie Uroff notes that there is 'a new factuality' in these poems, 'and a new attempt to see the landscape as a world endowed with her own bad spirits'.[5] The landscape of Plath's poem is reminiscent of an expressionist film image, as the sky 'leans' on her, darkness 'terrifies' the grass, and the 'black slots' of sheep's eyes seem to suck her into their depths. The opening lines are full of menace:

> The horizons ring me like faggots,
> Tilted and disparate, and always unstable.

Hers is a cruel landscape, populated by dirty, sinister sheep, and even the sky and the elements are oppressive. Hughes' poem is much less violent, much sadder. He contrasts the narrow world of Emily Bronte with all the possibilities still open to Plath. Looking at a photograph of Plath sitting in a tree, 'doing as Emily never did', he remembers the walk over the moors and remembers her vitality and her pleasure as an American ('your transatlantic elation') as she explored a famous literary scene. The comparison between the two poems is poignant: Hughes' poem, written years after Plath's death, focusses on the opportunities that were still open to her:

> The future had invested in you –
> As you might say of a jewel
> So brilliantly faceted, refracting

> Every tint, where Emily had stared
> Like a dying prisoner.

Plath's poem depicts a desolate landscape where bones whiten in the heather and buildings disintegrate. The fire that threatens to consume the world in Plath's opening lines returns in the closing lines of Hughes' poem, only here it is a flame of envy that is only gradually 'quenched in understanding'. Plath, like Emily, was a brilliant writer who died too young.

The American poems loosely follow the journey round the United States that Plath and Hughes made in 1959. The American landscape and its wildlife feature prominently, but through these poems the legacy of Plath's family history becomes more apparent. '9 Willow Street' contrasts what was happening in him when they moved into their apartment in Boston with the forces that a return home were triggering in her:

> And your heart
> Jumped at your ribs, you gasped for air.
> You grabbed at the world,
> For straws, for your morning coffee – anything
> To get airborne. My bubbles
> Wobbled upwards and burst emptily
> In the reverberations of the turbines
> Home and College had assembled in you

In this poem Hughes recounts the episode of how he saved a bat on Boston Common. He finds the creature, picks it up and as he does so, it turns savagely on him. Later, and only after the bat has bitten him does he remember that 'American bats have rabies'. The final lines of the poem draw an explicit parallel between the savagery of the American bat and the two poets' doomed marriage:

> How could Fate
> Stage a scenario so symbolic
> Without having secreted the tragedy ending
> And the ironic death? It confirmed
> The myth we had sleepwalked into: death.
> This was the bat-light we were living in: death.

Bats return in 'Karlsbad Caverns', where they are contrasted with the blindness that the two lovers suffer:

> Those bats had their eyes open. Unlike us,
> They knew how, and when, to detach themselves
> From the love that moves the sun and other stars.

The last line echoes the final line of Dante's *Divine Comedy*. For the poet and his wife there will be no escape from hell, no ascent into Paradise. In 'Child's Park' he makes this explicit:

> You were never
> More than a step from Paradise.
> You had instant access, your analyst told you,
> To the core of your Inferno –
> The pit of the hairy flower.

What is happening in these poems is that Hughes has begun to explore below the surface of events, to use the combination of his memories, of Plath's writings, often about the same scene or incident and his analysis, from a very different moment in time, of the significance of some of those moments. Inevitably, incidents acquire symbolic value with hindsight, and inevitably also he is constantly reminded of the abyss between what he thought he was seeing then with what he can see now.

Another of the American poems, 'The Blue Flannel Suit' takes up the theme of blindness and seeing. Looking back, Hughes understands what he could not see years before. He recalls Plath going off to teach, wearing a stiff, blue flannel suit. He knows now, as he did not know at the time, that she was suffering intensely, 'knowing yourself helpless in the tweezers/Of the life that judged you'. The suit, which he remembers both when he saw her wearing it and when he found it in her wardrobe after her death, becomes for him emblematic of 'a mad, execution uniform':

> Now, I see, I saw, sitting, the lonely
> Girl who was going to die.

One of Plath's most powerful poems, 'Electra on Azalea Path' finds its counterpart in 'Child's Park'. The opening line asks the basic question: 'What did they mean to you, the azalea flowers?' One answer to this can be found in Plath's *Journals*, where she records a visit to her father's grave at a time when she was watching her body carefully for signs of confirmation of her pregnancy. In Hughes' poem, the distance between him and Plath is portrayed in Dantesque terms. He sees her climbing a staircase, climbing into the mouth of an azalea flower in search of rebirth, a level of understanding that would bring her onto a new level of self-knowledge. 'You were fearless to meet your Father', he writes, through the use of the capital F, deliberately associating Plath's endeavour to find out more about her father and come to terms with his death with a desire to come closer to God. But the core of the flower is a nuclear zone. Just as Plath returns again and again to the image of the nuclear holocaust, so Hughes in *Birthday Letters* echoes that terror. She persists in her quest. He cannot cope:

> I stepped back. That glare
> Flinging your old selves off like underthings
> Left your whole Eden radioactive.

The final poem of the American sequence, 'Isis' marks a shift to a darker set of poems. Immediately after this poem comes 'Epiphany' that explicitly states that the marriage has failed. From this point onwards, the poems are increasingly full of foreboding and more violent images. The poem which follows 'Epiphany' is 'The Gypsy', in which a French gypsy outside Chartres Cathedral curses Plath with a prophecy that she will die soon. Hughes is horrified, but notes that 'you/went on writing postcards', as though the curse did not concern her. Later, after her death, he searches in vain through her diary for a mention of the curse. Had she heard what was said, he muses, or was she already closed 'in a solider crypt'? Had she already decided to die?

'Isis' is full of questions. The poem opens with the couple starting out to drive around the United States. The mood is optimistic:

> you had dealt with Death.
> You had come to an agreement finally:
> He could keep your Daddy and you could have a child.

His wife seems to have overcome her troubled past – 'Finally you had stripped the death – dress off,/Burned it on Daddy's grave'. The poet, her husband, feels that this time they are embarking on a new stage of the journey together:

Day of America's Independence
You set out. And I, not Death,
Drove the car.

But Death has not disappeared. The poet imagines Death as part of the luggage, a fellow traveller riding on top of the car or running in the shadow of the wheels. Death is described as 'waiting for your habits/To come back and remember him'. Not the drive around America, nor the pregnancy, nor the birth of a child can stop the inevitable recalling of Death. Tellingly, the poet notes that the moment came not in America but in England: 'Your blossom had fruited and in England/It ripened.' Images of childbirth and grotesque images of a ritual birthing of Death are juxtaposed, and the poem marks a shift into an increasingly dark world of mysticism, symbols and ritual sacrifice. Poetry and Death come together, and as Plath finds her powerful poetic voice, so she is represented as coming closer and closer to self-immolation. The driving force is, increasingly, her desire to be united with her dead father.

In 'The Minotaur' her father is represented as the beast, her children are abandoned in the labyrinth, while a skein of blood marks the unravelling of the marriage. In 'Brasilia', another poem that uses the same title as one of Plath's poems, Plath is portrayed as a destroyer; wearing her steel helmet like a demented gladiator, she decapitates father, mother and husband. Images of violence proliferate as the poems depict the disintegration of a marriage and Hughes hints at Plath's mental instability. The violent language of the poems mirrors that of Plath's own poems, and both poets transform ordinary items into objects of horror. One good example of this can be found in the transformation of a telephone into an aggressive instrument in Hughes' 'The Afterbirth' and Plath's 'Words heard, by accident, over the phone'. The narrative of Hughes' poem recounts how during the birth of their son at home, he caught the placenta in a bowl he used for preparing jugged hare and then buried it under an elm tree watched by his wife. But the last lines of the poem move to a bleaker scene. The poet remembers accidentally running over a hare, and writing about it later – 'it bled out of my pen'. The poem moves swiftly from birth to death as poetry, with the enigmatic figure of the hare, like a primeval god. The dead hare reforms on the poet's page, a hieroglyph of a hare:

You picked it up, curious.
And it screamed in your ear like a telephone –
The moon-eyed, ripped-up flower of it screamed.

In Plath's poem, the telephone is a hideous, tentacled monster that pours mud, spawn and excrement out of the earpiece, sowing seeds of evil. Many of the poems in *Birthday Letters* echo images from Plath's poetry, in a kind of counterpoint. The screaming telephone of Hughes' imagining mirrors the alien monster of Plath's; this echoing process happens ever more obviously in the poems in the latter part of Hughes' collection. Not only do many of Hughes' poems use identical titles to some of Plath's poems, but images recur and are woven into new patterns.

Many of the poems seek to analyse what was happening to Plath, part of an attempt to understand and come to terms with the past. 'Apprehensions' suggests that fear of losing all that was most dear to her was at the heart of Plath's existence, and that 'your writing was also your fear'. In 'Dream Life' a series of graphic images of destruction and horror pursue Plath from sleep into her waking life:

> When you did remember
> Your dreams were a sea clogged with corpses,
> Death-camp atrocities, mass amputations.

The birth of the children cannot assuage the terror. In 'Perfect Light', Hughes meditates on a photograph of Plath sitting with her new baby son, her face lit up 'like a daffodil', looking like a Madonna. The image of this beauty and maternal consolation however, is at odds with what the poet now knows. This short poem ends with an image of a battle-hardened infantryman returning out of no man's land, 'bowed under something'. This grotesque figure is the next moment of her life. Looking at the picture of his dead wife, with their two small children, captured on camera in what seems to be an idyllically happy instant, Hughes accentuates his sense of loss and failure.

In 'Suttee' he depicts himself as a midwife, helping his wife bring forth a child. But the labour is painful, the outcome horrible:

> And you had been delivered of yourself
> In flames. Our newborn
> Was your own self in flames.
> And the tongues of those flames were your tongues.

The destructive father figure, always present in *Birthday Letters* acquires evermore prominence through the volume. 'Suttee' equates father with husband:

And I was your husband
Performing the part of your father
In our new myth –

The narrative line through *Birthday Letters* presents the father-figure in increasingly diabolic light. The father is not only the destroyer, he is the enemy of both wife and husband, for it is on account of the unresolved terror and anger initiated years before by the loss of her father that Plath, in Hughes' version, turns on her husband. The first poems in the collection revolve around the gap between what the poet thought he knew and what he has since come to understand, but increasingly in the second half, after the America poems, the figure of the dead father rises like a vampire, bent on killing.

In 'The Cast' he is named again as Daddy, a reference to Plath's famous poem. Daddy has come back, to hear what his daughter had against him, and is depicted as unable to believe what he hears. As the words pour out, driven into him like a stake into a vampire's heart, he is transformed into a sacrificial figure, a Saint Sebastian pierced through with arrows. Killing Daddy is a symbol of the act of writing poetry. Mortally wounded, the Plath of Hughes' imagination struggles for deliverance from ancient pain. But even as she writes Daddy out, releasing the pain, a metamorphosis takes place:

Healed you vanished
From the monumental
Immortal form
Of your injury: your Daddy's
Body full of your arrows. Though it was
Your blood that dried on him.

The poet and her father are inseparable; she is possessed by him, so that killing him she destroys herself. This is the inevitable outcome predicted in some of the other poems. Death and poetry are seen as conjoined, the forces that release Plath's poetic talent are dark forces that eventually will destroy her, no matter how hard she struggles to survive. In 'Being Christlike', Hughes makes a series of bald state-ments about death and self-sacrifice, set down with a rhythm that is Biblical in its stress patterns. 'You did not want to be Christlike' is the sentence with which the poem begins and ends, but her desire to be with her father 'in wherever he was' drives her forward, even though her body bars the way and her family make it harder for her to get there. All the lines are crossing, her desire for her father, her poetry and her move towards death are depicted as coming together in a grim pattern of coherence.

Immediately before this poem is 'The Bee God', a piece that is to be read alongside Plath's bee poems. Here Hughes uses one of his favoured techniques of *Birthday Letters*: the blunt opening statement upon which the rest of the poem will be constructed:

> When you wanted bees I never dreamed
> It meant your daddy had come up out of the well.

Now he understands the link between her desire to keep bees and her dead father, and the poem juxtaposes statements about what he knows now with his ignorance at the time. Phrases like 'I never dreamed...I never guessed...I thought I was safe...' run through the poem. Plath is represented as a virgin goddess, making obeisance to the King of the Bees. Her husband cleans the old hive and paints it for her one summertime, thinking this will give her pleasure, 'but your bees/Had their own ideas'. The bees rush out in a savage swarm, and once again Hughes uses images of electricity – 'bees planted their volts, their thudding electrodes' – that connect with a host of real and imagined moments of destructive power: the electric shock treatment Plath herself received, the electrocution of the Rosenbergs, the electric forces used by Jove the Creator and destroyer in Hughes' version of *Tales from Ovid*. In this great force field he is powerless, and she, who has summoned up this power with her father can save neither herself nor him. Images of electricity run through *Birthday Letters*, and 'The Tender Place', one of the first poems in the collection is one of the most graphic poems on this subject, prefiguring the imagery of 'The Bee God'. After the shock, comes the aftermath: the poem ends with two poignant lines that 'translate' the last two lines of a poem by Plath. Hughes' poem concludes with

> Deaf to your pleas as the fixed stars
> At the bottom of the well.

Plath's poem, 'Words', ends with

> While from the bottom of the pool, fixed stars
> Govern a life.

As we progress through the poems in *Birthday Letters* quotations from Plath's poems increase, not as direct references but rather as hints and borrowings, as rewritings or translations. Daddy, the SS officer, the concentration camp guard, the archetypal German bogeyman is depicted as lying between husband and wife in 'The Table', planning with ruthless Prussian efficiency their destruction in 'The Bee God', a sacrificial victim in 'The Cast', a guttural-speaking corpse dragged into the light in 'Blood and Innocence'. But Hughes' version of 'Daddy' is necessarily different from Plath's, for in her poem 'Daddy' she explicitly connects father with husband. Her husband, the man she transforms into a new image of her father, has the same 'Meinkampf look/And a love of the rack and the screw'. In this poem, Plath seems to be fusing the two men in her life into a single, monstrous figure, so that both become vampires, both deserve punishment and, finally, both have stakes driven through their hearts. The poem ends with the death of the vampire and a scream of repudiation: 'Daddy, daddy, you bastard, I'm through.'

Hughes, of course, has a different version of the daddy story. Plath identifies him with her father, the ambiguity of her feelings for both men expressed through powerful images of violence. But Hughes appears to be trying to understand and come to terms with that history. 'Blood and Innocence' takes up another important theme that his poems develop – the desperation of Plath the bereaved child, the little girl whose father died when she was too young to understand and who has been haunted by insecurities and feelings of loss and abandonment ever since. In this poem, the image of the villagers dancing and stamping on the dead vampire that Plath creates in 'Daddy' is translated into a very different image, one that draws upon Germanic myth:

> Thor's voice its very self
> Doing a hammer-dance on Daddy's body,
> Avenging the twenty-year forsaken
> Sobs of Germania

The child-woman who has engineered this destruction looks round for approval, but finds herself in a 'gilded theatre' surrounded by faces

> Of Mummy Daddy Mummy Daddy –
> Daddy Daddy Daddy Daddy
> Mummy Mummy

and the poem ends with a child's desperate screaming for her parents.

The child is there again in a beautiful poem entitled 'Night-Ride On Ariel', one of several poems that make explicit reference to Ariel, both the character from *The Tempest* and Ariel as title of Plath's last collection. Daddy is here again in this poem, and so is 'your moon-mother', a figure who appears in many of the poems in *Birthday Letters* but who is never given the prominence she has in Plath's own writing, where the figures of both parents loom large. Hughes does not give so much space to mother figures in his poetry, probably because he is primarily concerned with exploring the ways in which Plath equated him with her father in her personal mythology. 'Night Ride On Ariel' is unusual in that Hughes names actual women who played particular roles in Plath's life – first of all, her own mother, then Ruth Beuscher, the Freudian analyst who explored the impact on the young Plath of losing her father and having a very possessive, ambitious mother, Mary Ellen Chase who arranged for Plath to have a teaching post at Smith College in 1957, Olive Higgins Prouty the novelist who funded the scholarship that took Sylvia Plath to Smith in the first place. These women are depicted as 'Phases/Of your dismal-headed/Fairy-godmother moon'. In their different ways, they manipulate the young Sylvia, who is overwhelmed by their 'criss-cross instructions' that pull her in different ways and eventually destroy her as she flies, like a female Icarus too close to the sun. The imagery of the poem echoes Plath's image of the fig tree in *The Bell Jar*, where she describes Esther Greenwood as being pulled apart by so many simultaneous aspirations. The last lines of the poem resonate with echoes from the last poems Plath ever wrote. The moon-women jam all wavelengths:

> Crackling and dragging their blacks
> Over your failing flight,
> Hauling your head this way and that way
> As you clung to the sun – to the last
> Shred of the exploded dawn
> In your fist –
>
> That Monday.

These lines take up the last lines of 'Edge', the final poem Plath ever wrote, where she depicts the moon as an old hag in mourning who has seen every kind of human suffering: 'She is used to this sort of thing/Her blacks crackle and drag'. The final lines echo the last lines of Plath's penultimate poem, 'Balloons' in which she creates the image of her baby son biting a balloon, then sitting back 'Contemplating a world clear as water', clutching 'a red/Shred in his little fist.' Mother and son, child and child-woman are joined together through this image.

With 'Life after Death' the poems in *Birthday Letters* reflect a move into a different, quieter phase after the violence and anguish of the sequence that leads up to Plath's death. Hughes writes about the banality of everyday life, as he feeds and dresses his motherless children, then draws upon images from fairytales of abandoned children in the depths of forests, comforted at night by the howling of wolves. The fox, the native animal that he has used as a symbol of poetic inspiration is replaced by alien creatures, by dingos and Brazilian-maned wolves, strange desperate creatures from another world. The poet depicts himself as a character from the Tarot pack, the Hanged Man, the twelfth figure of the Major Arcana, that comes just before Death. This is always seen as a card of great significance, but that significance has never been clearly explained by Cabbalists, which is presumably why Hughes chooses to use it here as an emblem of his tortured state of mind. The poem begins with a question that is never answered, because it cannot be answered.

In these last poems of the collection, memories of the past are expressed through a series of disjointed and fragmented images. The figure of Sylvia Plath dissolves surrealistically into body parts. In 'The Hands' his grief is expressed through images of empty gloves, hands and fingerprints, in 'The Prism' he recalls his wife's earrings and her 'sloped brown shoulders' as she walks towards the sea, in 'Freedom of Speech', where he imagines a sixtieth birthday party for a Plath who did not die and who has resolved all her inner conflicts, he mentions her knuckle and her lips. Fingers and lips return in 'Fingers', and in all these poems the motif of dismemberment is used as a powerful way of expressing the disjointedness of grief and the disjuncture between past and present, between what was remembered as having happened at the time and what is remembered with the added knowledge of Plath's version of the same events. There is a great quietness in these poems and a great sense of weightiness.

One poem in particular, 'The God', reflects this change of mood. This poem is almost a summary of everything that has gone before, a resumè not of Plath's actual life but of her life as a poet. A metamorphosis has taken place, and the angry wife has become the creative genius, the flesh and blood woman has become a terrifying priestess of a strange, death-bringing god. The characteristic statement with which the poem begins tells us that:

> You were like a religious fanatic
> Without a god – unable to pray.
> You wanted to be a writer.

Then comes the crucial question – 'What was it within you/Had to tell its tale?'. The poem struggles to answer this terrible question, through images of fearsome religious rites that the speaker cannot understand. The poem is full of references to other dark gods and their rituals, to the Aztec god who demanded human sacrifice, or the cruellest manifestations of Christianity. The 'writer's god' orders his acolyte to write about her tortures, he burns and torments her, but she devotes more and more of her life to his service, offers him yet more sacrifices:

> You fed the flames with the myrrh of your mother
> The frankincense of your father
> And your own amber and the tongues
> Of fire told their tale. And suddenly
> Everybody knew everything.

As she transforms her life into poetry, exploring the darkest recesses of her memory and turning her innermost secrets into words, so she becomes 'a trance-dancer' round the altar, oblivious to everything else in her life, to the child-god she has given birth to, to the man who nursed her in her pain. The flames burn higher, 'God is speaking through me' she tells her husband, who begs her not to go on: 'Don't say that', I cried. Don't say that./That is horribly unlucky.' The poem ends in a crescendo of horror, as she is consumed by the flames while her helpless husband can only stand by and watch. The explosion of fire consumes everything, as the writer's god is also transformed:

> you
> Vanished, exploding
> Into the flames
> Of the story of your God
> Who embraced you

And your Mummy and your daddy –
Your Aztec, Black Forest
God of the euphemism Grief.

'A Picture of Otto', a much quieter poem, draws upon the familiar episode of classical writing of an encounter with the dead in the underworld. Hughes imagines a meeting with Plath's dead father, imagines his shock at what his daughter has done to him in her writing and at the way in which she imagined both men as one and the same:

Your ghost inseparable from my shadow
As long as your daughter's words can stir a candle.
She could hardly tell us apart in the end.

This bitterly ironic tone, however, masks a message not of resignation but of acceptance. 'I understand' says the poet, acknowledging that he like Plath's father is what she has made of him and neither of them can change that. But there is a growing sense in these poems of something emerging from the wreckage of the marriage and the untimely suicide. Through his memories, her beauty endures, as it also does through her children. In 'Fingers' he writes:

I remember your fingers. And your daughter's
Fingers remember your fingers
In everything they do.
Her fingers obey and honour your fingers,
The Lares and Penates of our house.

Plath has become a goddess, but not the destructive goddess of some of the earlier poems, she is the quiet goddess of her children's household. The next poem, the penultimate poem in the collection 'The Dogs Are Eating Your Mother' opens with another of Hughes' typically bald statements: 'That is not your mother but her body.' This is the message that *Birthday Letters* proclaims, that Plath endures through her poetry and through her family and their memories of her. The references in this poem are to the repeated desecration of her grave by feminists outraged by the inclusion of the name 'Hughes' on her headstone. For years after Plath's death, Hughes was reviled as having driven her to take her own life, and the repeated desecration of her headstone is evidence of the strength of feeling against Hughes felt by many women who saw Plath as a feminist icon. The inclusion of this poem in the sequence hints at the personal distress felt by Hughes and his children during the years when he was publicly vilified, and reflects the careful organisation of the poems in the collection. These final poems are about memory, but they are about a different kind of remembering than that which is the subject of many of the earlier poems. Whereas those poems juxtaposed what the poet remembers with how Plath herself wrote about the same incidents and experiences, leading him to question the validity of memory, here the poems have a more affirmative tone. The poet no longer questions himself or his dead wife, he has come to accept that forces beyond his power led to her death. What is left to him are traces of her, that live on through their children and through their respective poems.

The last poem of *Birthday Letters* is entitled simply 'Red'. It is a poem that develops once again the great contrast between husband and wife, only here that contrast is expressed in terms of colour. Plath's own colour symbolism led her to use white, black and red, the colours of the Triple Goddess in her poetry. Hughes focusses on her use of the colour red, both in symbolic and literal terms. Red is the colour of poppies and roses, of salvias, the flower after which she was named, it is the colour of blood. 'You revelled in red', Hughes writes, remembering her red velvet skirt, her bright red lipstick, the red carpet and upholstery she chose for their home. The poem opens with a statement: 'Red was your colour'. It is the colour she could not avoid, the colour of 'the heart's last gouts,/Catastrophic, arterial, doomed'. He depicts her as trying to escape the inevitability of redness, but always failing:

> Everything you painted you painted white
> Then splashed it with roses, defeated it,
> Leaned over it, dripping roses,
> Weeping roses, and more roses,

Yet in this compulsion that pulls her towards death and its colour, there is a sign of hope. Painting blood-red roses that obliterate whiteness, sometimes, 'among them, a little bluebird'. The bluebird is the symbol of joy, and in the last lines of the poem Hughes celebrates the colour blue. 'Blue was better for you' he writes, remembering the blue silk she wore during her pregnancy:

> Blue was your kindly spirit – not a ghoul
> But electrified, a guardian, thoughtful.

Electricity, the blue spark is not destructive here, it is beautiful. Blue, the colour of the sky and of bluebirds' wings is the colour with which Hughes chooses to close his memories of Plath. The poem ends with the word 'blue':

> In the pit of red
> You hid from the bone-clinic whiteness.
>
> But the jewel you lost was blue.

The whiteness of bones and the redness of blood give way to the tranquil colour blue, just as the violence of Hughes' recollections has ended with acceptance of the past and recognition of continuity beyond death.

In the third act of *A Midsummer Night's Dream*, Bottom the weaver is changed by Puck into a man with an ass's head. His companions flee in terror, and as he runs, Peter Quince cries out 'Bless thee, Bottom! bless thee! thou art translated.' The term 'translated' as it is used here carries within it different layers of meaning, most significantly the idea of transformation. It is this notion of translation that underpins *Birthday Letters*. The poems are much more than a retelling of a tragic story from the husband's perspective, much more than an exercise in setting the record straight. The volume is organised in such a way that we are led through a transformative process, a translation as it were. On one level, the story of two lovers who came together and then divided in the most painful of circumstances is told through the poems, but on another level the volume traces the development of a great poet, a woman whose gift was nevertheless to lead to her own destruction. In this respect, *Birthday Letters* is a translation of Plath's life and of her legacy and we see her undergoing a series of metamorphic processes that end on a note of sadness and tranquillity.

Deliberately woven into the fabric of *Birthday Letters* are words, phrases, titles taken from Plath's own poems. One of the most beautifully poignant poems is entitled simply 'Error', and here we can see the translation process clearly. The poem tells a simple story, that of the destruction of different dreams. The opening line states, 'I brought you to Devon. I brought you into my dreamland.' The poet acknowledges his responsibility for having made a wrong choice. In the beginning, he describes his wife as coping loyally, 'gallant and desperate and hopeful', trying to integrate into a strange community, 'stripping off/Your American royalty'. The mood darkens, the English landscape is awash with rain, the house rots 'like a coffin' and the gulf between husband and wife grows wider. Half way through the poem comes the single line: 'This was Lyonnesse', and straight away there is connection with Plath's poem, 'Lyonnesse', a connection that becomes increasingly strong as words, phrases and images are reworked. Plath's poem focusses on the death of a marriage, the end of the dream of Camelot. Hughes' poem similarly traces the end of the marriage, but does so through Plath's version, picking up words and translating them in different ways. The 'round bubble' that rises from the mouths of drowned people and cows in Plath's poem recurs in Hughes' as he looks back: 'Remembering, I see it all in a bubble'. He transforms her cows into bullocks, sunk in mud, emblematic of the end. But whereas her poem is built around shifting, abstract images, his is firmly rooted in the reality of the sodden, autumn countryside. The two poems operate in counterpoint with one another, and to appreciate either of them fully, it is important to read both.

'Error' can be considered as a translation of 'Lyonnesse', for it effectively rewrites Plath's poem and, like any good translation, moves the original on. Translation, as Walter Benjamin argues, offers a continuation of life to an original text, enabling that text to reach a new generation of readers in another place and another time.[6] The idea of translation as after-life, as continuation, perhaps even resurrection is a powerful one, and one that sees the activity as essentially life-enhancing. Hughes, in *Birthday Letters*, gives us a version of Plath's life and writing that can truly be described as life-enhancing, for he gives new life to her reputation, as a poet and as a human being.

Notes

All references and quotations used in this book are taken from the *Collected Poems*, ed. Ted Hughes (London, Faber & Faber, 1981).

TRACING A LIFE

1. Karen V. Kukil (ed.), *The Journals of Sylvia Plath 1950–1962* (London, Faber & Faber, 2000). Entry for July 1950, p. 9. All subsequent citations are from this edition.
2. This and all subsequent citations of the letters are taken from Aurelia Plath (ed.), *Letters Home* (London, Faber & Faber, 1975).
3. Lois Ames, 'Notes Toward a Biography' in Charles Newman (ed.), *The Art of Sylvia Plath: A Symposium* (London, Faber & Faber, 1970), pp. 155–174.
4. Ibid., p. 162.
5. Sylvia Plath, *The Bell Jar* (London, Faber & Faber, 1966), p. 250. First edition published in 1963 by William Heinemann, London.
6. 'America! America!' in Sylvia Plath, *Johnny Panic and the Bible of Dreams* (London, Faber & Faber, 1977), pp. 40–45.
7. Margaret Dickie Uroff, *Sylvia Plath and Ted Hughes* (Urbana, Chicago, London, University of Illinois Press, 1979).
8. Journal entry for Summer, 1951, p. 87.
9. Journal entry for March, 1961, pp. 606–607.
10. A. Alvarez, *The Savage God* (London, Weidenfeld & Nicholson, 1971), pp. 5–34.
11. Ann Sexton, 'The Bar-fly Ought to Sing' in Charles Newman (ed.), 1970, pp. 174–182.
12. Mary Kinzie, 'An Informal Check-list of Criticism' in Charles Newman (ed.), 1970, pp. 283–300.

POETRY AS PROCESS

1. Journal entry for 12 December 1958, pp. 436–437.
2. Journal entry for 21 February 1958, p. 335.
3. Appendix 2, Journal entries June 1957 to June 1960, p. 612.
4. Appendix 15, Journal entry for 7 June 1962, pp. 656–657.
5. Susan van Dyne, *Revising a Life: Sylvia Plath's Ariel Poems* (Chapel Hill and London, University of North Carolina Press, 1993).
6. Journal entry for 15 November 1959, p. 530.
7. John Frederick Nims, 'The Poetry of Sylvia Plath' in *Arien Ascending: Writings about Sylvia Plath* (New York, Harper & Row, 1985), p. 46.
8. Nims, op. cit., p. 46.

9. Ted Hughes, Introduction to Sylvia Plath's *Collected Poems* (London, Faber & Faber, 1981), p. 13.
10. Ibid., p. 16.
11. Ibid., p. 14.
12. Journal entry for 20 March 1959, p. 475.
13. Sylvia Plath, *The Poet Speaks* (Argo Record Co. No. RG455 Lm. 1962).
14. Margaret Dickie Uroff, *Sylvia Plath and Ted Hughes* (Urbana, Chicago, London, University of Illinois Press, 1979), p. 13.
15. Ted Hughes, 'Sylvia Plath and her Journals', in *Ariel Ascending*, ed. Paul Alexander (New York, Harper & Row, 1985), p. 153.
16. Ibid., p. 162.
17. Lucas Myers, *Crow Steered Bergs Appeared: A Memoir of Ted Hughes and Sylvia Plath* (Sewanee, Tennessee, Proctor's Hall Press, 2001), p. 100.

GOD, NATURE AND WRITING

1. Suzanne Juhasz, *Naked and Fiery Forms. Modern American Poetry by Women: A New Tradition* (New York, Harper & Row, 1976), p. 90.
2. Sylvia Plath, 'A Comparison', broadcast July 1962, pub. in *The Listener*, July 1977. Reprinted in *Johnny Panic and the Bible of Dreams* (London, Faber & Faber, 1977), pp. 62–65.
3. Ted Hughes, 'Notes on the Chronological Order of Sylvia Plath's Poems' in *The Art of Sylvia Plath*, ed. C. Newman (Bloomington and London, Indiana University Press, 1970), pp. 187–199.
4. John F. Nims, 'The Poetry of Sylvia Plath: A Technical Analysis' in *The Art of Sylvia Plath*, ed. Charles Newman, pp. 136–152.
5. Sylvia Plath, *The Poet Speaks* (Argo Record Co., No. RG 455 Lm., 1962).
6. Margaret D. Uroff, *Sylvia Plath and Ted Hughes* (Urbana, Chicago, London, University of Illinois Press, 1979), p. 63.
7. *Letters Home* adapted by Rose Leiman Goldemberg for performance by two actors, playing Sylvia and Aurelia Plath.
8. See note in *Collected Poems*, p. 275.
9. Michael Riffaterre, *The Semiotics of Poetry* (Bloomington and London, Indiana University Press, 1978).
10. Sylvia Plath, 'Context' in *Johnny Panic and the Bible of Dreams*, op. cit., pp. 98–99.
11. 'A Comparison', op. cit., see Note 2.
12. Judith Kroll, *Chapters in a Mythology: The Poetry of Sylvia Plath* (New York, Harper & Row, 1976), p. 21.
13. *The Bell Jar*, p. 80, see Chapter 1, Note 11.
14. Robert Graves, *The White Goddess* (London, Faber & Faber, 1961), pp. 446–447.
15. Mary Jacobus, 'The Difference of View' in *Women Writing and Writing About Women*, ed. Mary Jacobus (London, Croom Helm, 1979), p. 14.
16. Suzanne Juhasz, op. cit., p. 102.
17. Ann Sexton, 'The Barfly Ought to Sing' in *The Art of Sylvia Plath*, ed. C. Newman (Bloomington and London, Indiana University Press, 1970), pp. 174–181.

WRITING THE FAMILY

1. References here are to David Holbrook, *Sylvia Plath, Poetry and Existence* (London, The Athlone Press, 1976). This book is an example of the worst kind of Plath criticism, also see A. Alvarez, *The Savage God* (London, Weidenfeld & Nicholson, 1971). Although interesting and full of personal insights, Alvarez' perceptions of Plath are steeped in sexist self-indulgence.
2. *The Bell Jar*, p. 65, see Chapter 1, Note 11.
3. Ibid., p. 234, see Chapter 1, Note 11.
4. Journal entry for September 1951, p. 98.
5. Carole Ferrier, 'The Beekeeper's Apprentice' in *Sylvia Plath, New Views on the Poetry*, ed. Gary Lane (Baltimore, Johns Hopkins Press, 1979), pp. 203–218.
6. Note to 'The Disquieting Muses' in *Collected Poems*, p. 276.
7. *The Bell Jar*, pp. 215, 233, see Chapter 1, Note 11.
8. Adrienne Rich, *Of Woman Born* (London, Virago, 1977), p. 230.
9. Preface to *Johnny Panic and the Bible of Dreams* (London, Faber & Faber, 1977), pp. 18–19.
10. *The Bell Jar*, pp. 176–177, see Chapter 1, Note 11.

WRITING OUT LOVE

1. *The Bell Jar*, p. 241, see Chapter 1, Note 11.
2. Suzanne Juhasz, *Naked and Fiery Forms* (New York, Harper & Row, 1976), p. 88.
3. Margaret D. Uroff, *Sylvia Plath and Ted Hughes* (Urbana, Chicago, London, University of Illinois Press, 1979), Chapter IV, 'Plath's Cambridge Manuscript', pp. 63–84.
4. Judith Kroll, *Chapters in a Mythology* (New York, Harper & Row, 1979), pp. 248–251.
5. 'The Wishing Box' in *Johnny Panic and the Bible of Dreams*, op. cit., pp. 100–111.
6. 'The Fifty-Ninth Bear' in *Johnny Panic and the Bible of Dreams*, op. cit., pp. 100–111.
7. Ted Hughes, 'Notes on the Chronological Order of Sylvia Plath's Poems' in *The Art of Sylvia Plath*, ed. Charles Newman (Bloomington and London, Indiana University Press, 1970), pp. 187–195.
8. Robert Graves, *The White Goddess* (London, Faber & Faber, 1961), pp. 367–368.

POETRY AND SURVIVAL

1. Ted Hughes, note in *Encounter*, October 1963.
2. A. Alvarez, *The Savage God* (London, Weidenfeld & Nicholson, 1971), pp. 28–29.

3. *The Bell Jar*, p. 1, see Chapter 1, Note 11.
4. Ibid., p. 250, see Chapter 1, Note 11.
5. Preface to *Johnny Panic and the Bible of Dreams* (London, Faber & Faber, 1977), p. 15.
6. Sylvia Plath is included in the section entitled 'Where Are the Women Playwrights?' in *Women in American Theatre*, eds Helen Krich Chinoy and Linda Walsh Jenkins (New York, Crown Publishers, 1981).
7. Eileen Aird, *Sylvia Plath* (London, Oliver & Boyd, 1973), p. 14.
8. 'Sylvia Plath' in *The Poet Speaks*, ed. Peter Orr (London, Routledge & Kegan Paul, 1966), pp. 167–172.
9. Susan R. Van Dyne, 'More Terrible Than She Ever Was', 'The Manuscripts of Sylvia Plath's Bee Poems' in *Critical Essays on Sylvia Plath*, ed. Linda W. Wagner (Boston, G. K. Hall and co., 1984), pp. 154–170.
10. Anne Cluysenaar, 'Post-culture: Pre-Culture?' in *British Poetry since 1960: A Critical Survey*, eds Michael Schmidt and Grevel Lindop (Oxford, Carcanet Press, 1972), pp. 219–221.
11. Margaret Dickie Uroff, *Sylvia Plath and Ted Hughes* (Urbana, Chicago, London, University of Illinois Press, 1979), p. 169.

PLATH TRANSLATED: TED HUGHES' *BIRTHDAY LETTERS*

1. Elaine Feinstein, *Ted Hughes, The Life of Poet* (London, Weidenfeld & Nicholson, 2001), pp. 231–232.
2. Lucas Myers, *Crow Steered, Bergs Appeared: A Memoir of Ted Hughes and Sylvia Plath* (Sewanee, Tennessee, Proctor Hall Press, 2001), p. 34.
3. Eilat Negev, *My Life with Sylvia Plath*, by Ted Hughes, *The Daily Telegraph*, Saturday, 31 October 1998, p. 4.
4. Ted Hughes, *Poetry in the Making* (London, Faber & Faber, 1970), pp. 20–21.
5. Margaret Dickie Uroff, *Sylvia Plath and Ted Hughes* (Urbana, Chicago, London, University of Illinois Press, 1979), p. 216.
6. Walter Benjamin, 'The Task of the Translator' (1923) in Walter Benjamin, *Illuminations* ed. Hannah Arendt, trans. Harry Zohn (New York, Schocken Books, 1969), pp. 69–82.

Bibliography

SELECTED WORKS BY SYLVIA PLATH

Ariel (London, Faber & Faber, 1965; New York, Harper & Row, 1966).
The Bell Jar (London, Heinemann, 1963; Faber & Faber, 1966; New York, Harper & Row, 1971).
The Colossus and Other Poems (London, Heinemann, 1960; New York, Alfred A. Knopf, 1962; London, Faber & Faber, 1967).
Collected Poems (London and Boston, Faber & Faber, 1981).
Crossing the Water (London, Faber & Faber, 1971; NewYork, Harper and Row, 1972).
The Journals of Sylvia Plath, eds Ted Hughes and Frances McCullough (New York, The Dial Press, 1982).
The Journals of Sylvia Plath 1950–1962, ed. Karen V. Kukil (London, Faber & Faber, 2000).
Johnny Panic and the Bible of Dreams and Other Prose Writings (London, Faber & Faber, 1977).
Letters Home, ed. Aurelia Plath (New York, Harper & Row, 1975).
Uncollected Poems (London, Turret Press, 1965).
Winter Trees (London, Faber & Faber, 1971; New York, Harper & Row, 1972).

SELECTED WORKS ABOUT SYLVIA PLATH

Books listed here are those which the author has found useful. Some more extreme interpretations of Sylvia Plath's life and work are noted in the endnotes but are not listed here. Most books in this list contain useful bibliographies, giving details of where to find individual articles, stories, poems and so on by Sylvia Plath, also reviews and articles about her work.

Aird, Eileen, *Sylvia Plath* (New York, Harper & Row, 1973).
Alexander, Paul (ed.), *Ariel Ascending: Writings about Sylvia Plath* (New York, Harper & Row, 1985).
Alexander, Paul, *Rough Magic: A Biography of Sylvia Plath* (New York and London, Viking, 1991).
Alvarez, A., *The Savage God* (London, Weidenfeld & Nicholson, 1971; New York, Random House, 1972).
Bronfen, Elizabeth, *Sylvia Plath* (Plymouth, Northcote House, 1998).
Butscher, Edward, *Sylvia Plath: Method and Madness* (New York, Seabury Press, 1976).
Butscher, Edward (ed.), *Sylvia Plath: The Woman and the Work* (New York, Dodd Mead, 1977; London, Peter Owen, 1979).
Holbrook, David, *Sylvia Plath: Poetry and Existence* (London and Atlantic Highlands, NJ, The Athlone Press, 1976).

Homberger, Eric, *A Chronological Checklist of the Periodical Publications of Sylvia Plath* (Exeter, Exeter University Press, 1970) (American Arts Pamphlet No. 1).

Hughes, Frieda, *First Pressings* (London, Faber & Faber, 1998).

Hughes, Ted, *Birthday Letters* (London, Faber & Faber, 1998).

Kroll, Judith, *Chapters in a Mythology: The Poetry of Sylvia Plath* (New York, Harper & Row, 1976).

Lane, Gary (ed.), *Sylvia Plath: New Views on the Poetry* (Baltimore and London, Johns Hopkins University Press, 1979).

Lindahl-Raittila, Iris, *From Victim of the 'Feminine Mystique' to Heroine of Feminist Deconstruction. Auto/Biographical Images of Sylvia Plath, 1963–2001* (Åbo, Åbo Akademi University Press 2002).

Melander, Ingrid, *The Poetry of Sylvia Plath: A Study of Themes* (Stockholm, Almqvist and Wiksell, 1972).

Myers, Lucas, *Crow Steered, Bergs Appeared: A Memoir of Sylvia Plath and Ted Hughes* (Sewanee, Tennessee, Proctor's Hall Press, 2001).

Newman, Charles (ed.), *The Art of Sylvia Plath: A Symposium* (London, Faber & Faber, 1970; Bloomington, Indiana University Press, 1970).

Rose, Jacqueline, *The Haunting of Sylvia Plath* (London, Virago, 1991).

Saldivar, Toni, *Sylvia Plath: Confessing the Fictive Self* (New York, Peter Lang, 1992).

Steiner, Nancy Hunter, *A Closer Look at Ariel: A Memory of Sylvia Plath* (New York, Harper's Magazine Press, 1973; London, Faber & Faber, 1974).

Stevenson, Anne, *Bitter Fame: A Life of Sylvia Plath* (London, Viking, 1980).

Uroff, Margaret Dickie, *Sylvia Plath and Ted Hughes* (Urbana, Chicago and London, University of Illinois Press, 1979).

Van Dyne, Susan R., *Revising a Life: Sylvia Plath's Ariel Poems* (Chapel Hill and London, University of North Carolina Press, 1993).

Wagner, Linda (ed.), *Critical Essays on Sylvia Plath* (Boston, G. K. Hall and Co., 1984).

Wagner, Linda, *Ariel's Gift: Ted Hughes, Sylvia Plath and the Story of Birthday Letters* (London, Faber & Faber, 2000).

Wagner-Martin, Linda, *Sylvia Plath: A Biography* (London, Chatto & Windus, 1987).

Index